DAVID SPANIER

The Hand I Played

A Poker Memoir

Oldcastle Books

First published in 2000 by Oldcastle Books,
18 Coleswood Road, Harpenden, Herts, AL5 1EQ
www.highstakes.co.uk

A CIP catalogue record for this book is available from the British Library.

ISBN 1–84243–006–8

2 4 6 8 10 9 7 5 3 1

Typeset by Palimpsest Book Production Limited,
Polmont, Stirlingshire
Printed by Omnia Books Limited, Glasgow

For Gideon, Joshua and Samson
Sons and Players

'The smart money was on Goliath'

CONTENTS

Preface

If one is in love with a game, and then devotes the time and energy to write about it at length, the result will be a book such as this. David Spanier captures in *The Hand I Played: A Poker Memoir* many of the forces that have shaped this most egalitarian and cerebral form of gambling, and which have driven poker's transformation from its plebeian roots to its current status as an emerging participant and spectator entertainment form that now commands a modicum of respect.

Spanier looks at poker – and occasionally the broader gambling scene – from a variety of perspectives. He draws from his own experiences as a lifelong amateur player and mild poker fanatic, providing anecdotes that have poignant messages, such as the pain and anxiety he felt as a schoolboy being in debt to the bookies, and having to explain such circumstances to his conservative and god-fearing parents. He brings his personal involvement to the present with the Tuesday night poker game – a game at which in earlier years many of the competitors across the table ended up writing their own poker memoirs (i.e. Al Alvarez and *The Only Game in Town*, Tony Holden and *Big Deal*) – and with the important new phenomenon of net poker. In his chapter 'Tuesday Night', Spanier captures the cerebral dimensions of the game, the banter among males who are both aggressing and regressing, and ultimately makes the point that such play might really be an important part – the highlight perhaps – of its participants' lives.

This is a memoir that looks at the life, experiences

and insights of the author, David Spanier, through the observant eyes of the poker player. But it is about more than just poker, as Spanier draws from his lifelong experience as a journalist, author, teacher and philosopher to create an entertaining and instructive treatise on how life is like poker, and poker is like life.

Spanier as journalist has covered the most visible staged poker event – the World Series of Poker at Binion's Horseshoe in Las Vegas – virtually since its inception nearly 30 years ago. His role expanded to his own participation in the tournament – where his $10,000 entrance fee was sponsored by an 'angel' from the Tuesday night game – in 1997. He captures the event's spirit, following an informal observer/participant methodology, in a manner that is both engaging and instructive.

Spanier as teacher provides insights into the dimensions that make poker interesting, strategic, and challenging. His discussions of particular hands or situations convey a sense of understanding as to why people become fascinated, even obsessive, with poker. One also gains insights as to why the poker game of Texas Hold 'em has evolved into the game of choice among many serious and most professional poker players. In the chapter, 'Cruisin'', where Spanier was given a free berth on a Caribbean cruise ship in exchange for lectures as a poker instructor (figuratively singing for his supper), he observes the unusual and eccentric sociology of people who are attracted to poker cruises, and of passengers whose typical preoccupation is not the next port-of-call or the passing scenery, but rather the hand they played last night or last year that they should have won.

Spanier as philosopher makes some important fundamental points about poker as a slice of real life. Regardless of how good you are as a player, you can always step up in class – typically measured by the size of the wagers permitted – and you can find yourself overwhelmed by more skilful players (e.g. if, after five minutes, you don't know who the sucker at the table is, it's you.) Poker is also the great equalizer. The rocket scientist or brain surgeon who cannot disguise a 'tell' can easily fall prey to the ditch digger or retiree who can spot one. "It means that any player can sit down with any other player – duke or dustman, millionaire or shoe clerk – on the same terms . . . At the table it is *how* everyone plays that counts." Poker indeed is both a test of skill and an examination of character.

Spanier is generally recognized as one of the premier journalistic authorities on gambling and commercial gaming in the world. He has a well-established reputation as an *aficionado* of and expert on the game of poker, having written a regular poker column for the *Independent* in London, and contributing on gambling subjects to such publications as the *International Herald Tribune*, the *Financial Times*, and the *Daily Telegraph*. He also had a long career as a foreign correspondent for *The Times* of London. He managed to be viewed simultaneously as a distinguished and erudite London journalist with considerable credibility and insight, and as a formidable Las Vegas poker player with a funny accent, wearing a baseball cap, who was known at the table as 'Dave.'

In *The Hand I Played*, Spanier takes on a topic that is expanding as part of popular American, as well as British, culture. Poker has always had a place in the American landscape but, as with Las Vegas and casinos, it was usually relegated to the more socially opprobrious categories. It has only been in recent years that poker has begun to be seen with less – though still somewhat – jaundiced eyes, and it is attracting a cult following not unlike professional wrestling, but with more direct participation, and fewer body slams.

Sadly, David Spanier did not live to see this book come into print. While playing poker at the Grosvenor Victoria Casino in London on an April night in 2000, David was stricken ill. Within two days, he had died of a brain haemorrhage. Coincidentally, word had just been received that the University of Nevada Press had decided to publish *The Hand I Played*, and the American version of his other recent book, *The Little Book of Poker*, had just been released by Huntington Press.

At the time, David had much to look forward to in his personal and his professional life, and it was with no small irony that he should meet his end the way he did. He was one of those people with ongoing plans for the future that he looked forward to with excited anticipation. He also never had a sick day in his life – or so he claimed – and aren't we all supposed to be around for the next festivities, the next big conference, the next World Series, the next big deal?

It was not to be, and so David moved off the stage and into the memories of those who knew, loved, and respected him. This book is therefore his last testament, and a continuation of his formidable spirit. He will be missed.

William R. Eadington
Series Editor, Gambling Studies Series
University of Nevada Press
Professor of Economics
University of Nevada, Reno

1

Rambling 'n Gambling

You gotta know when to hold 'em, know when to fold 'em
Pop song *The Gambler* as sung by Kenny Rogers

She woke me from a deep sleep at 4.30 a.m. with a question.

"Are you a compulsive gambler?"

And this, after twenty-six years of marriage.

I kept my eyes resolutely shut. "Wha'? Wassa matter?" I mumbled, turning over.

"But *are* you?"

"Um . . . talk about it in the morning . . ."

The trouble had started the previous evening. We had dinner at our neighbourhood restaurant with an old friend, Bill Eadington, Director of the Institute for the Study of Gambling and Commercial Gaming at the University of Nevada, Reno. Afterwards, I had driven him back to his hotel, and then slipped off for an hour – no more! – of poker at the Victoria casino.

I was back home in bed, where she was already asleep, by midnight. This had offended matrimonial propriety in some way.

But compulsive? Unh-hunh, forget it.

My trouble is the other way round. I can't really bring myself to gamble. Can't let go. I know too much about gambling to fling my money around.

Of course, I had learned the hard way. Don't we all?

My fascination with gambling began at Charterhouse, one of the top-drawer public schools for boys. It was a fairly harsh institution when I first went there, just after the war. Institution is the right word for it. Set on a fine wooded hill outside Godalming in leafy Surrey, the school – on the face of it – was a close-knit, high-spirited community of teenage boys, getting an education in the traditional British middle-class way. In those post-war years, the school was driven by a relentless ethic of team spirit. Sport was the measure of talent and popularity. Boxing was compulsory. Gruelling cross-country runs set the pattern – the Pontifex, five and a half miles long, up hill and down dale, we covered in 45 minutes plus. The junior training corps, one afternoon a week, included boots, drill, rifles, field days in the wild, and an annual camp.

These recreational activities were slotted into an elaborate system of fagging and school privileges. As a 'new hop' you had to learn various improbable bits of information about the school and the masters such as 'The science beak has a cork bottom'. You were not allowed, as I recall, to do up the middle button of your tweed jacket until your second year, and so on and so forth. All this was regulated by a scale of punishments, rising all too rapidly to regular beatings with a cane by the head boy of the house, if not the headmaster. Smoking was a serious offence, which if repeated led to instant expulsion.

Yet it all seemed good clean fun! We didn't know any other way of doing things, had no other standard of conduct to measure it against. The showers were not cold, the food was not too bad, the school tuckshop, facing the First XI cricket ground, was a den of delight, selling ices and currant buns. There were no girls, of course. Instead, boy-on-boy friendships (the word gay had not then been purloined) formed the staple of school relationships, and led to continuous, overheated tittle-tattle.

Some things change for the better. Today's school is unrecognisable from what it was. It has become much, much milder, freer and open to intellectual and artistic pursuits. Nothing could illustrate the change more graphically in the mid '90s than the headmaster, poor fellow, being obliged to resign after he was betrayed to the tabloid press by a cheap tart he had picked up in a massage parlour . . . in the nearby town of Godalming! Might as well imagine a jukebox on Parnassus.

This was the background against which I discovered gambling. I do not want to dwell on the mindless and extremely unpleasant anti-Semitism which prevailed at Chouse (as we abbreviated the school name), which undercut my enjoyment of my time there. School life was sport, sport, sport all the way, football, cricket, hockey; fives, squash; athletics; swimming, shooting; inter-house competitions at all ages, five days a week. Indoors, in my house, we played endless games of desk football, flicking pennies and halfpennies, big-sized coins back then, with a wooden ruler so as to propel a silver sixpence, serving as the ball, across the table. I joined in all these sports with huge enthusiasm. I must have been in my second year, aged fourteen, when bookmakers' ads in the newspapers first attracted my notice.

In those days betting on horses was a quite a complicated thing to do. There were no betting shops. Credit accounts were for the rich. Street corner betting via bookies' runners was illegal, though flourishing in London and elsewhere. Instead, betting by post was the way to do it. I selected a firm in Glasgow called J. John, stuck a ten bob note (equivalent to about £11 in today's terms) and sent it off with my selection. Whether the first bet won or lost I don't remember, but it certainly whetted my appetite for playing the horses. I would select a runner or two from the morning paper, enclose my stake and mail the letter off. The postmark was the guarantee it was a genuine bet made before the off.

I won a few and lost a few but what I recall most clearly was the day when J. John got its sums wrong, in failing to calculate my winnings properly. I wrote a very stern letter saying that such a mistake was unacceptable behaviour on the part of such a distinguished firm as J. John.

They put it right. The bookmaker in Glasgow had no inkling, naturally, that Charterhouse might be a boys' school and this particular punter under age. When they paid me out with blue Scottish pound notes, as they sometimes did, I got rid of them on future bets. I think that another boy and I even subscribed to a tipster in a racing paper. This kind of betting, I suppose, was an escape route from school and a sort of external recognition of my individuality. No harm was done, financially speaking.

My second memory of betting on horses is less agreeable.

In the school holidays, still aged about fourteen or fifteen, I formed the habit of walking down from Hampstead, where we lived, to Golders Green to a bookmaker's and going in, accompanied by our cocker spaniel, to place a bet or two. In this instance, the two men who ran the firm knew perfectly well I was under age, but they went on taking my bets. Half way through the holidays I had a little run and found myself some £13 or £14 in credit. Whereupon, they turned on me, quite nicely, and demanded to know if I was under twenty-one.

They said they could not, in these circumstances, pay me. It would be illegal. They bore me no ill-will, adding (I remember this detail) that they liked dogs, especially my cocker spaniel. This pair of oily bookies certainly risked losing their licence if word got out that they had been taking bets from minors, but I did not realize that. I did not want to be reported to the police or face trouble at home.

I hurriedly accepted their claim that being under age I could not make bets and therefore could not be paid, and backed out with the dog. I recall being so upset when I got back home that I told my mother I did not want lunch. This was so surprising a turn that I soon found myself confessing what had happened. She took it calmly. I ate lunch after all.

I would not say I had become hooked on betting on horses, but this experience left me with the (false) impression that I could beat the book. Also with a nasty taste about the probity of bookmakers. Still, I do not think I punted very much through my teenage years, until I had gone in and out of military service and arrived at Cambridge University. Here my betting life took a dramatically different turn.

A group of us would meet for lunch in a Cambridge pub where the talk, most days, centred on what was happening at Newmarket (known as 'headquarters' among racing men). One of the regulars at the pub was an older man named Jack Catterall, a big, red-faced, hail-fellow-well-met sort of chap, who drove a horse van and had a job supplying feed to racing stables. He was a ready source of insider tips, which sometimes went right and sometimes went wrong. For instance, he had a tip about a horse called Rough, which was supposed to win. We backed it and it lost. Then when Rough ran again, and Jack did not back it, the horse won at 20–1. A disaster.

At that time we noticed a curious feature of *The Times*, which was then a newspaper of record, of high seriousness, with no news on the front page – and miles better for it. (I suppose it was around then that I hit on the idea that I wanted to work for *The Times* when I went down from university.) Anyway, the *Times'* racing coverage was markedly different from all other newspapers, whose racing correspondents proffered naps and tips and 'good things' every day of the week. *The Times* simply offered a bare list of selections. But once in a while, without any fuss, the *Times'* man would write, after the name of the horse he chose, the brief phrase "—is a confident selection." His confidence was very nearly always justified. And we began to wait for these special days, which were few and far between. So far between, in fact, that we were rapidly led to betting on all manner of other tips, good, bad and indifferent. Of course most of them lost. But what did that matter? When you are young and carefree and living on a sufficient allowance from your father, gambling on horses is as right and natural as a baby's smile.

We placed the bets by phone with a local bookie, on credit. He knew we were foolish undergraduates and did not seem worried about our getting into debt and failing to pay on time, which we all did, habitually. But every time things got dark and overdrawn, along would come another winner to bale us out, or nearly so, which meant we could begin the cycle of betting and losing and 'kiting' cheques (writing out a cheque and hoping to make enough money to clear it by another bet coming up) all over again. What fun! I don't regret a moment of it – apart from one moment, that is.

Inevitably, I got deeper and deeper into debt. I don't remember what my father gave me as my term's allowance in those dewy-eyed days, when a good meal in a restaurant probably cost a pound and a hardback book half a crown. Whatever my allowance was, a hundred pounds or so after rent and college meals, I ran through it pretty quickly and got more and more heavily into debt with our friendly local bookie.

By then I had one or two credit accounts with London bookmakers too, which by contrast did have to be settled on time. Just how far I had got into debt I can remember by a little incident (how these things stick in one's mind) when Jack Catterall tipped a horse called Eastern Emperor, on which I placed the huge sum of £100 (say £1,600 today). It won at 3–1. I was sitting in the barber's shop the next morning when Jack's cheery red face appeared round the door. "And how's the Eastern Emperor?" he inquired jovially. The answer was that the Emperor was still stuck, even after that big win.

And so it went on, despite tipsters' letters, newspaper naps and even the occasional 'confident selection'. Another day older and deeper in debt. Finally, one spring day when Cambridge was at its most magical, the sombre realization was borne in upon me that I was going to have to own up and tell my father. As a stockbroker who ran a small family firm, he was himself the epitome of financial probity and good sense. I knew this betrayal of trust by me, his elder son, would upset him profoundly. Not for the money, which – a matter of a few hundred pounds – he would understand and pay off at once, but for the shame of letting him down and all that.

Still, I had to go through with it. There was no alternative. I had bills to pay at college and in town and the local bookie was getting less friendly by the week. I could not, and did not want to, refuse to pay up. I feared the story would get out to my tutor, with whom I had already had one or two mild mishaps, such as returning from Cheltenham races with Jack Catterall after the college closing hour of midnight. My safe, carefree little world as an undergraduate was crumbling beneath my feet. So I resolved, and it was a difficult decision to make, to tell all to my father. "I am sorry to have to tell you, Dad, I've been a bit foolish . . ."

I chose the moment for this confession to be a weekend when I had to return to London for a family party – a birthday or wedding anniversary. This was the right time. I travelled back on the train with a doleful heart. In one sense, I knew this sort of youthful peccadillo had happened countless times before, and did not really matter; but in another sense I was deeply ashamed of the pain I was about to cause. The family party took place in an atmosphere of high celebration. Saturday night turned into Sunday morning. Now was the moment of truth, or moment for truth; during a walk on Hampstead Heath before Sunday lunch.

But I put off the moment. The party had been so successful, the whole family was in such high spirits, I could not bear to puncture the happy atmosphere. We were a very close family, my dear mother and father and two boys, and grandmother. I judged that making my confession after lunch, just before catching the train to Cambridge, would be less painful for all of us.

Then in the afternoon, as the post-prandial mood lingered on, I thought again. It was not, I told myself, funk or moral cowardice. I took a clear and calm decision that I would not wreck the weekend in the way I knew I was bound to do. I would spare my father and mother that unhappy ending, and do the deed another time. After all, what was the difference in putting it off another week? The debt would still have to be paid. So I returned to my college rooms in Great Court, Trinity, looking out on the most beatific of all English quadrangles, guarding my guilty secret to myself. I knew I had done the right thing.

And then a curious thing happened. A day or two later in the pub, another tip came up. It was in fact no more than a longish priced nap by another newspaper tipster. I was so far in that one more bet made no difference, so I stuck £50 each way on the horse. The bookie didn't like it but he could not turn down the bet and risk giving me an excuse not to pay my account. I did not even buy an evening paper that afternoon to look at the results, because I had already written off the wager as soon as it was made. Amazingly, miraculously, the horse won at 7–1.

Even this was not enough to clear my account but it was more than enough to relieve the pressure. I rang the bookie next day, explained I would pay off the rest of what I owed him as soon as I could, and told him to close my account. So far as gambling was concerned, this episode – getting into debt, going back home and not telling my parents, and then getting out of it by an unexpected stroke of luck – was the shaping experience of my life. I did not give up gambling but I was seriously chastened. I resolved never again to get so far in that gambling could threaten my whole life. We all have to learn our lesson and it is better to learn it young.

Jack Catterall was not so fortunate. Some months later he took his own life because of his gambling debts. All we knew about it was a bleak paragraph in the *Cambridge Daily News*. He had left a note protesting that the bankruptcy court, in its unrelenting campaign against him, had driven him to suicide.

Around this time I got involved in another side of gambling which rapidly became my favourite game, the avocation I was known by and, finally, the theme of my career in writing: poker.

Our poker school grew out of our horse racing. We were an assorted bunch: Peter Scaramanga (wonderful name) who was a louche sort of layabout, old beyond his years; David Whitby, straight up, son of the then Vice-Chancellor of the University; a man called George Tamer, a charming Lebanese of good family, whom I lost touch with; Michael Alexander, whose family transport business in Scotland had been nationalised (one night he confided what they got "Tew mill-yun!" for it) and Guy Packer, a tremendously lively cockney sparrow, full of jokes, who had ridden the winner of the classic race the Cesarewitch as a youngster of seventeen, and was now getting too heavy to be a jockey.

We played five card draw, jacks to open, with enthusiasm and no judgement. A win of a tenner was a big swing. We had a circle of girlfriends and hangers-on, we gambled, we drank to excess, we celebrated youth in ancient Cambridge as youth should be celebrated. What happened to them all? Where are the poker players of yesteryear?

Poker suited my temperament. Here was a game of skill, of amusing companionship, which still had a big gambling element in it. Naturally, we continued to play the horses and we roistered all night and all the rest of it. But poker became a special pleasure for me, a pleasure distinct from all other pursuits. Down the years poker has opened doors for me, enabling me not just to win money but to meet all kinds of people, high and low, to play in Las Vegas and other resorts, to become an author, and eventually to devise an alternative profession (from being a diplomatic correspondent) as a journalist. It is still far and away my favourite occupation and recreation. Could one ask for more?

After graduation, the Cambridge game continued in London in a new form, with new players, based on an enticing, candle-lit, little restaurant called Le Rêve, in King's Road, Chelsea. It was the threshold of the 'swinging sixties'. Le Rêve was run by a bevy of sassy young women who were filling in the pre-career or pre-marriage gap with casual jobs. They all became friends and lovers of us players. We would eat and drink at Le Rêve till closing time and then head back to a flat close by in Paulton Square, where one of the founders of the game lived, one David Gillies. Even in his undergraduate days, Gillies was a cultivatedly dissolute young man, who chose, deliberately, to squander his talent as a writer in nihilistic drinking. But he shared my passion, at this time, for poker.

The game was dealer's choice, with all kinds of wild cards and twists, played for stakes far beyond our means. That is what poker in your twenties is all about – jousting, like would-be knights at arms, across the baize, daring fortune. Another player was Alan Williams, who made a hit as a thriller writer before he also fell to drink. Then there was Peter Townend (always cool, sun-tanned, a stud playing up his movie-star looks) and a motley group of hangers-on – journalists like Peter Jenkins, political columnist of *The Guardian*, and BBC broadcaster Richard Kershaw; young sprigs from the City like Richard King (who later ran Majestic Films International), anyone who could be roped in. I was by then working as a reporter on *The Times*, leading (I suppose) a double life.

Since the stakes were far too high and the games ran all night, we were always in debt to each other. I remember, for instance, one night when a casual acquaintance, owner of a string of steak-houses, played in the game, and lost the huge sum, in those days, of £1,000. The following week he managed to win £12, and we had to struggle, the rest of us, to dig up the cash to pay him! That was how it was.

Meanwhile, the girls at Le Rêve were drawn to our little school like fireflies. I think we had romantic entanglements with all of them but, *au fond*, poker took precedence. You know the ritual – the build-up before the game, telephone calls and assignations to round up the players; dinner at Le Rêve, good talk over cheap wine. Then back in the flat, the poker table a-gleam with piles of chips, crisp decks of new cards; the wild and weird variations succeeding one another through the night, the patchwork of credit and cheques in trying to settle up, the drive back to bed in the light of dawn; the post-game calls on the phone later in the day, the re-runs of big hands; and the warm-up to the next Friday night game . . . youth, youth!

Around this time, I got involved in two other games, which show the extraordinary social reach of poker. One was at Crockford's, the gambling club in Carlton House Terrace; the other, only five minutes away, was a café in the Strand, called the En Passant. This was a working-class caff doing coffee and egg-and-chips, which attracted chess players of all sorts and standards. They crammed the far end of the long narrow room of the En Passant, oblivious to everything except the game in hand – chess players, as I can vouch for from my lifelong enthusiasm for the royal game, are even more addicted than poker players. The charm of the En Passant was that upstairs, in a little attic, hidden from view, was a floating poker game which ran all day and all night and never seemed to stop. It attracted a cross section of low-life players, hustlers and hangers-on, who dropped in and out, for as long as they pleased or could afford.

It was up here that I learned, as all players have to do, the hard grind of poker, the ins and outs of the game which make it so much more subtle than the mere rules of play, which look so simple. Did I win? Well, sometimes. My accent gave me away as a bit of a toff and, therefore, an easy mark. On the plus side, I was not desperate for money, unlike most of the players up there, playing off their beam-ends. That upstairs room was a warm, intense, scruffy, very enclosing and comforting space to be in, an easy retreat from the cares of day-to-day living.

The games were not always straight. Five card stud is a game which lends itself to cheating because the identity of one card is so crucial. But even the cheats were not very expert. It was a game where people stayed for nights and days on end, or until they 'did' their money. One of the traditions of the En Passant, instituted by Ted Isles, who ran the game, was GHM or Going Home Money. When a man went broke, as most players were bound to do, he was given a hand-out of a couple of quid to take a taxi or a bus back home. There were some tragic cases of people going broke.

One I remember in particular was a young man who came in two or three days before Christmas and despite many pleas and protestations to the contrary, managed to do all of the money painstakingly saved up by his girl back home, intended for Christmas dinner and his baby daughter's presents. When he finally lost his last few bob, he was really done for. Not even a decent wad of GHM could have saved him, because he would simply have gambled it away elsewhere. Probably unconsciously, he wanted to break with his domestic life, but what a shameful way to do it.

Amid all the betting and bluffing and 'strokes' there were fights and rows, friendships made and broken, small fortunes won and lost – all human life, as the famous newspaper phrase put it, was there. Ted's partner, the man who ran the café, was a large, lugubrious, heavy-eyed type called Boris Watson, a softly spoken and educated man, possibly of Russian origin. He played chess well and poker badly. Once I was rash enough to invite him along to my other game, the one we played after dinners at Le Rêve. Boris could see we were all mugs but the game was so complicated – seven card high low with a twist, plus wild cards – he could not get hold of it, and lost £500. Of course the predictable happened. His cheque bounced.

I went along to the En Passant and remonstrated with him. Boris shrugged and shilly-shallied. He could not pay even if he wanted to. It was my own fault. You should never invite players to poker games without being absolutely sure they can afford to pay if they lose. But you always do invite them anyway, because the school, on a particular night, needs another player to make up the game. I nicked one of Boris's chess clocks as token compensation, and drove up to Cambridge to play a few games with the don who, a few years earlier, had directed my studies in English. Curious, by the way, how this delightful and learned man, Theo Redpath, who had taken Ph.Ds in law, English and music, who translated both Sophocles and Tolstoy and was a friend of Wittgenstein, could never, for the life of him, manage to play chess. The same thing probably applies in poker – mere learning, culture or IQ seem to have no direct or obvious correlation with winning.

Another *habitué* of the En Passant was Colin Kennedy, who was also a Cambridge graduate but who played, by contrast, very well. He had a maths degree and was marked by a fearfully spotty complexion. He had (as the current expression has it) dropped out. Why? "Because I like playing poker a lot better than getting a job," Colin told me in his pawky Scots way. Colin played well enough to back up Ted or Boris by running the game when needed. This meant cutting the pot, keeping a close eye on everything going on, and still managing to play his own hand and win. Colin was (and is) a strong player who has over the years won a lot more money, tax free, than he could have expected to make as an accountant or actuary or whatever maths graduates do for a living. He has got, so he believes, far more satisfaction from playing cards than following a regular career.

I was never tempted to go that way. For one thing, I did not play nearly well enough to survive as a professional. And for another, I had a career. I liked journalism and always will. It is a calling which gives you a thrill and a challenge every day and an extraordinary degree of freedom in how you work. What I was able to do, though I did not foresee it back then, was to parlay my enthusiasm for poker into my journalism, so that I could write about the game.

In the early 1960s when I was posted by *The Times* to Brussels as Common Market Correspondent, I used to fly back at weekends and dive into the En Passant to pick up on the regular games and the gossip. Someone once recalled this saturnine figure, in a coat with a velvet collar, arriving in a flurry with a briefcase stuffed with papers, cigar in hand. Not quite! I never had a coat with a velvet collar. The En Passant of blessed memory could not last for ever, unfortunately. The place was pulled down for rebuilding and Boris, who had fallen on hard times, tried his luck as a numismatist, selling coins under the name of John Copperman. He died, I fear, a disappointed man.

His partner at the En Passant, Ted Isles, was tougher. He was not exactly without mercy, but he was a hard man. GHM was handed out to the deadbeat losers in dribs and drabs, reluctantly, if not grudgingly. (Rather like the old *viatique* system at Monte Carlo, when destitute players would be paraded around the Principality, so that everyone could mark them down as uncreditworthy, before being sent back home on a train.) Ted was an ex-policeman who had spectacularly fallen off the beat. Instead of taking a sixteen-year-old girl in his charge into custody, he had chosen to seduce her. Bravo! Ted's heavy style is shown by a little trap I set for him one night, of no real consequence. Making change of a pound note for him, I deliberately paid him 21 shillings. He counted the money down and did not bat an eyelid, sliding the coins into his stack.

A hard man but more or less fair, Ted was living with Liz, a light, bright, pretty girl who was clearly middle-class, and sounded it, in sharp contrast to his own resolutely working-class style, which took its tone from the criminal fringe. Such liaisons, across the classes, were unusual in the England of those days. Liz would sit around the poker room, making tea or coffee, chatting amiably, passing the hours of her days and nights, but never playing. Once I tried making a pass at her to see if it would ruffle Ted. No reaction whatsoever!

After the En Passant came to an end, Ted continued to run games here and there, usually from his pad in Soho, trying to eke out a living. The games were too irregular to prosper, but the wide circle of punters who had made a life or found a refuge in the En Passant, like old boys keeping in touch with their public school, kept dropping in. The survivors of those days still feel a bond.

Tom Wolfe caught the style of the En Passant exactly:

"The top floor is the poker room, and it is like a big garret. It is gloriously seedy. There is some kind of wall-to-wall carpet on the floor, only it doesn't look like a carpet but like the felt padding you put under a carpet, and it is all chewed up and mouse-grey with bits of cigarettes and lint and paper and God knows what all else all caught in the chewed up surface. There is more haze from the smoke, and at the end of the room there are six men seated around a table, playing poker, under a big lamp with a fringe on it. They are all in their 30s and 40s, it looks like, a couple in very sharp sort of East End flash suits, like Sharkskin's, a couple in plain off-the-rack-suits, one in kind of truck-driver clothes, and one guy looking rather Bohemian, in some kind of trick zip-up shirt of corduroy."

Wolfe's droll piece described how when the fire brigade was called to the building, neither the chess players downstairs nor the poker players upstairs paid the slightest attention.

"With a tremendous crash one of the fireman, ax in hand, breaks through the kitchen window. He stares at the six players, concentrating on their cards, and all of a sudden feels a bit sheepish.

'I think I broke some of your teacups when I came through the window,' he says.

'Woooooooeerrrrr' says Sharkskin, 'why don't you get in the game, and we'll take some readies off you.'

The fireman walks over to the table and looks at the punters with their pile of 'readies'.

'Wooooeerrrrr,' he says, ax in hand, 'I think I'll just watch.'"[1]

It was no surprise when Ted came to see me one day and asked to borrow a few readies. I let him have £500

[1]Tom Wolfe's Britain, *Sunday Telegraph Magazine*, November 28, 1966.

in return for a series of post-dated cheques, the last of which bounced. By then I had been posted by *The Times* to Washington and could not collect. When I got back to London I managed, with some difficulty, to wheedle it out of him. Ted was a force of nature so far as poker and money were concerned. You just did not expect to get it off him.

A while later I repeated my mistake and made him another loan. He had a child to support and I knew he needed the money. Besides, Ted had, in my eyes, a saving grace. He was a very strong chess player, one or two of his games even featured in chess anthologies. Ted was getting older and pastier and had lost his enthusiasm if not his hard edge. The games had faded. He was overweight and followed a dissolute life. He went and died before the loan was repaid. As I say, you couldn't beat Ted. He always got the best of it, even in death.

The game which had the most influence on me, I suppose, was at Crockford's. My introduction to it came in a roundabout way, through a casual friendship with the later-to-become-world-famous Lord Lucan. In those days, when his father held the title, his name was simply John Bingham. John's parents lived in the flat above my family in St. John's Wood but I was always too shy of approaching him.

Then unexpectedly, one balmy June night at the casino at La Croisette in Cannes, I saw him playing *chemin de fer*. In his early thirties, wearing a white dinner jacket, his hair swept back over his noble brow, his gaze calm, languid and assured, he looked the epitome of an aristocratic sprig whiling away a night at the gaming tables. John affected the same expression of mild amusement whether he won or lost each coup, as the shoe went round. I introduced myself, we had a drink and we became friends. Back in London, I got to hear of the poker at Crockford's, the celebrated and long established card club, then located in a stately mansion in Carlton House Terrace. This must have been just a year or two before the Gaming Act of 1968, regulating casinos. I invited John to come and inspect it with me.

We were greeted by a splendid scene. The whole room, high-ceilinged, sparkling under chandeliers, seemed to be filled by old ladies, Jewish grandmothers predominant, furiously engaged in playing five card draw. They played intensely, very fast – shuffle, cut, deal; bet, raise, call! – because the table charge was, as I recall, a pound or two an hour, and they did not want to lose a moment of their precious time. The hands were played out with machine gun rapidity. The ladies were not so old, I realize now, as they appeared to our youthful eyes. But we were certainly young. We shone out, the pair of us, like milk teeth.

And the old ladies played well – they were not only fast but full of guile. The pace of the game was relentless. On one occasion, after inquiring if it was my turn to bet and being told it was, I murmured as I looked down at my cards "I see . . ." when the dragon opposite me snapped: "You see do you? Queens-up! Thank-you-very-much," raking in the chips. The great thing about Crockford's was that you could drop in for an hour before supper or stop by late, and always find the room full of eager old ladies. Lose? Of course we lost. Who wins in the card clubs, anyway? Apart from one or two smart players, the house is the big winner.

John introduced me to the Hamilton Club, which was

a town house at the end of Park Lane (now rebuilt) where in gentlemanly, but slightly decaying grandeur, they played five card draw and deuces wild and other simple variations. The Hamilton was a classier, less frenetic version of Crockford's, with plenty of action. John became the centre of a fast-living set of men-about-town, including a couple of high-rolling stockbroker types. All that was way beyond me, but I do recall one surreal evening when a very old, very gay gentleman called Captain Solomons or some such incongruous name – I am not sure if he didn't even wear a monocle – invited me and John to dine with him and his equally decrepit companion.

They must have known we were not of their sexual bent. But to be seen dining out with a real lord, of such fresh and aristocratic mien as John, set them purring like a pair of old cats. I remember only one line from that evening when the Captain told me, in a confidential aside, that once a week he had a young man come and visit him in his flat. "Just once a week, you know." I wasn't sure if this was an invitation for one of us to follow suit or just a confession of faith. We returned rapidly to the card game.

Although I was never close to John, in due course I attended his wedding and he attended mine. I liked him for his drawling, generous, easy-going manner and, above all, his love of cards. One night we were cheated in a game somewhere and he took it without complaint. In fact, as I have written before, I never met a player who won, or lost, with such good grace. All that was long before his crack up: his drinking and his debts, the break up of his marriage, and finally the terrible night his children's nanny was brutally battered to death, and Lucan subsequently charged with her murder.

I do not myself believe he is alive, press speculation to the contrary. My reason is quite simple. If he disappeared, as he did, to protect his children, surely his only reason for continuing to live on would have been, one day, to come out of hiding and stand trial, so as to see his children (now grown-up) once again. He has shown no sign of life since that fateful night of his disappearance. Had he done so he would by now have been a free man, with plenty of friends, such as casino owner John Aspinall, to ease him back into gaming society.

Many years, and much speculation later, Taki, the celebrated columnist of High Life in the British weekly *The Spectator*, wrote a curious little paragraph in his gossip column in the *Sunday Times*. In the context of another, quite separate, story about the late James Goldsmith, Taki remarked, in a small subordinate clause, that Lucan had died the day after the murder. This flat statement, a throwaway line written without any elaboration, went unremarked. Certainly I had never seen it before. It was categoric. Taki knows.

At Crockford's I got involved in horse racing betting again. A clever Indian player called Nonhi had developed a system for betting on two-year-olds. Unlike all other systems I have come across, this one worked. The basic idea behind it was to back two-year-olds, each-way. The form was very reliable and if the horse did not win it almost invariably got placed, saving the win stake – this was in the days before betting tax. Naturally, the bookmakers hated this way of betting. Bookies are looking for punters who give them 'value', that is, back horses all and sundry, every day of the week, without fear or judgement.

Nonhi's problem was that none of the bookies with

whom he used to hold accounts would take his bets any more. He and his partner needed two or three people like me to help them get their money on. In return, I had reliable information about which horses were worth backing, to make my own bets. Although I had to place only small amounts for Nonhi, like £3 or £4 each-way, it was still very difficult to get the money on. The bookie's telephonist at the other end of the line would huff and puff and groan and go away and come back and, if I was lucky or had had a couple of losers that week, grudgingly accept the bet. I had to ring around a lot. The system was not sensational, it yielded a profit of about 35 to 40 points in a flat racing season. But, as I say, it did work.

Then the day came when I got a two line letter from the biggest bookmaker in the country, William Hill. I kept the letter, because I was very proud of it. It read:

27th July, 1972
Dear Sir,

We thank you for your letter dated the 25th instant.

Owing to the Levy, Betting Tax and other increasing overheads, we regret we are no longer in a position to accommodate your type of business.

Yours faithfully

WILLIAM HILL (Park Lane) LIMITED

A.C.Enright.
Accounts Manager.

Right on! So now you see why I treated my wife Suzy's

question in the middle of the night, "Are you a compulsive gambler?" with such sleepy disdain.

My poker apprenticeship continued in Washington where I was sent by *The Times* as (God save us) US Economics Correspondent. I knew as much about economics as you could write on a fingernail, but no matter. The great attraction of the National Press Club on 14th Street, where all the press bureaux were located, was that on the top floor they had a poker game every lunch time.

What joy! No need to run around making sure there were enough players, no need to worry about food or drink – the game was on, every day of the week. We played very low stakes, as I recall $2–$4 five card stud, which was called for some reason 'rootles'. My English accent, which sounded so bizarre to a lot of the correspondents from outlandish provincial papers, made them doubt that I could really play the all-American game. My obvious enthusiasm rapidly established me as one of the guys. No one played very well, it was all fun.

Most engaging of all those players was Bob Coyne, who was some sort of lobbyist for the liquor industry. When he went out West on his travels I used to tease him he was trying to corrupt the Mormons. Bob was the ideal kind of poker player you sometimes come across – always open and positive, always amused and amusing, never complaining when he lost. After suffering a run of poor cards, he would announce, like proclaiming the Declaration of Independence: "Low card theory!", informing the table he was playing up a card like a five or a six in the hole. On another occasion I remember him standing up to go home after a very bad session and saying simply, "Thanks for the lesson!" – a perfect valedictory remark, which I have often employed on my own account. A poker table inscribed in Bob's honour was installed in the card room while he was still an active player – a fine tribute to his life.

Why did grown-up men spend so much time playing low-rent five card stud? Why does anyone play these kind of games, one might ask. The answer is not that we were all boys at heart but that, hell, it's good to get away from your desk and your typewriter and just gamble a little bit. Time enough, in the rest of the day, for serious stuff. The deadline for the first edition of *The Times* in London was about 2 p.m. Washington time, so I had to file pretty fast, in order to get to the table when the game started. I usually did.

I did not gamble, beyond the occasional bet on a heavyweight boxing match, and felt no urge to gamble. This period was only a few years after my débâcle at Cambridge and, evidently, I had learned that lesson. But, when, I ask myself now, a whole generation older, did I become such a tight player? Not in those days of 'low card theory' and wild card variations in private games, such as I sometimes played with Joe Rogaly and John Graham, the Washington correspondents of the *Financial Times* (up in their office!). It must have been back in London when I organised a new Friday night school, made up of journalists and other media people.

Yes . . . that must have been when I saw that simply by playing tight and waiting for good starting hands I was pretty well sure to win. And win big at the stakes we played. In an obvious sense this is the essence of poker; starting with the best cards. But in another way, you have to *play* your cards, especially in private games, and show that you will take chances, and give other players chances. If they come to feel they will never get it off you ("You'll need a crowbar!" Lucan used to joke) you become rather unpopular. Drawing this fine line between winning and playing a bit loose I have never found easy.

This led to the worst experience of my poker life. Not losing, but being barred from the game – blackballed, as they would say in the gentlemen's clubs of Pall Mall. Our Tuesday night game had been running for I don't know how long, ten years or perhaps longer. As poker games do, it had survived week after week, through thick and thin, with the same hard core of players augmented by occasional players from out of town. The game was famous, far beyond our locale, thanks to the writing of people like Al Alvarez and Tony Holden and myself.

We played a feisty high stakes game (too high for our own good, which was the root of the trouble) of dealer's choice. The money went around. You could easily win or lose £3,000 which was for us middle-class journalists and freelance writers, with young children to educate, a lot of moolah. I was never the big winner. But I was, at the end of each year, never a losing player either.

All of us, as happens in poker games, were quite close friends away from the table. We had wined and dined in each others' houses and had celebrated and commiserated together over love affairs or other personal matters. But they resented my style, playing so tight. I would sometimes try and loosen up, and play hands I would not, in cold judgement, want to bet on. But such good resolutions to 'try harder', as they say in school reports, did not last very long.

So it happened, and I remember the night precisely,

during the Falklands War of 1982, the night when a British warship had been hit by an Argentine missile and took serious casualties. I had been working late at London Broadcasting, where I was diplomatic correspondent, commenting on the war every day, almost hour by hour. I arrived at the game an hour or two after it had started. I then took a telephone call at the game, as I recall actually playing a hand as I responded to a question on air, explaining some new development. I certainly did not feel like playing poker and got tighter and tighter. Late on, a hand of seven card stud came down and I folded high-showing cards, for a paltry bet of a couple of pounds, which really anyone would have normally played. Someone, a newcomer to the game, expostulated:

"What is this, David? This is supposed to be a friendly game! Aren't you playing anything except aces! Jesus Christ!" And so on. There was a murmur of assent all round.

"Sorry, I had nothing," I said, turning over my hand. There was an ominous silence. "I don't feel like playing tonight, with all this Falklands stuff, I'm going home. Send me a cheque for my winnings tomorrow," and I left.

Somehow I knew this was a watershed – I had had warnings before. In the morning I rang Alvarez and he suggested I should take a couple of weeks' break from the game. There was a tradition in the Tuesday game of discussing key issues, such as what to do about a long-running debt from an ex-player or the suitability of a new player, before the game started. They discussed my case the following week.

Then I got 'the letter', as it became known. Written in impeccably polite terms, with a strong undercurrent of regret, it informed me I had been formally banned from the game. O-U-T. My tight play, they all understood, was simply my style and they knew I couldn't change my spots. The trouble went beyond my own play: it was having a very bad effect on the whole game, in effect seizing up the others, and making them all play too tight. I had to accept, in my heart, that the letter was justified. I took it without rancour or dissent, bad as I felt at the time.

I remained on reasonably friendly terms, away from the poker table, with all the people involved. For instance, in Vegas where we went every year for the World Series, Tony Holden and I spent a lot of time together, sometimes talking about our private life (outside of poker) in a way which we would never have done back home. I found other games to play, such as in the Victoria casino. Al Alvarez advised me that I was better suited to these club games, where you can play as tight as you damn well want, and would probably enjoy them more, and he was quite right.

That was how the position remained, for about four years. I was out of the game, though I heard what was happening and knew who was up and who was down, mainly via Paul Haycock who was very loyal to me. It's curious that Paul, who is a doctor turned pharmaceutical director and a very solid guy, is the only person I ever met through publication of my book *Total Poker* (1977) who became a close friend. Then, I don't know how it happened, the climate changed, there was a sort of move to bring Spanier back. I went to see the inner group of three or four players, and convinced them I could change my spots, and I came back into the Tuesday game as if I had never been away.

Several more years of the Tuesday game went by, week in and week out, during which I not only tried to play looser, but sometimes lost some big hands from doing so.

And then the same thing happened again!

I was co-organiser of the game, with John Moorehead who was easily the big winner in the game (he had no other real occupation). One year, he reputedly won close to £50,000, and one night, at my house, he dropped £10,000 – which took some doing. We took it in turns rounding up the players, getting the food in and hosting the game, which always ran till about 3 a.m. or later, and somewhat disrupted domestic life.

Our aim was to keep the game going, at all costs. So it happened that four weeks in a row we were down to four players. None of us really wanted to play short-handed, but that was how it was. As luck, or tight play, would have it, I won £1,000 on each of those four weeks, which was not a bad result. On the fourth week, a little hand came up around midnight, one player bet and I folded a worse card. He was furious, protested and said it wasn't worth going on playing like that. The game broke up early, which was unprecedented.

I was off to Las Vegas that week and away for ten days or so. I wasn't unduly concerned, because another player in that foursome was, as we all knew, even tighter than me. They could hardly ban me and leave him in, I thought. But when I got back to London, I was given the bad news. *Out.*

This time I did feel resentment at my treatment. I had done everything right, held the games at my house, played loose, never complained when losing, and generally been a good sport. I went to see the man who had objected to my play on the night in question. He was a photographer who had sort of got lost in the swinging '60s and never found himself again, a likeable fellow but given to taking very strong and inflexible views about the game – his nickname was 'Rules'. He was adamant. He would not be moved in any way. This time I was out for the count.

I felt awful. To be turned down by your peers, is there anything worse, from a social point of view? Yet in a funny way it wasn't personal. This time, in any case, I knew there could be no return. And then two very nice things happened, which immediately relieved my gloom. First, I was invited by my favourite newspaper, *The Independent*, to contribute a weekly column on poker. This was my long-cherished ambition in life. I mean some people want to climb Everest or sail around the world single-handed or drive a racing car at Le Mans. I wanted to write a poker column in a national newspaper. (And as far as I know it was not only the first, but remains the only such column.)

Secondly, an old friend Victor Lownes, former director of the Playboy Club, about whom I had written in the famous 'casino wars' in London in the 1980s, suddenly rang me up. "Come on over," Victor said, "there's a seat open." That is how I joined the Wednesday game. This game, which I still play in, was much more fun than the Tuesday game – new variations, low stakes, amusing company, hosted by George and Fiona Hacker (herself an excellent player). Later it was George who put me up to play in the World Championship in Las Vegas.

So instead of playing on Tuesdays, I played on Wednesdays. That's the way it goes, and I can truthfully say I don't pine one little jot for the old Tuesday game whose original happy-go-lucky spirit, as it turned out, more or less evaporated. Looking back, this whole episode of my poker life, which went on and off for years, seems like a bad beat which came good.

I got involved in the Grosvenor Victoria casino. It was, it is, a big glittery dump of a place, cheap, cheerful and down-market, situated in the middle of the Edgware Road. It is a very ethnic casino, appealing to a voluble bunch of Greek Cypriots, assorted Middle Easterners, Indians in turbans, Africans in robes, Americans on vacation, the whole mix well salted with a strong flavour of cockney low life. No wonder the club rule is 'English only at the table'. It might seem an odd place to become the centre of my poker life.

To begin with I found the poker a bit uncongenial, but gradually I got into it. I got to know all the players, as only a journalist can. And as someone who writes about the game – not that many Victoria club patrons bother with a paper like the *Indy* – I had a unique position at the club.

What appealed to me was the weird cross section of players. I am a good listener and pretty well everyone in the poker room has talked to me at one time or another. My motive, to start with, might have been to get a line on my opponents, which is normal poker technique. But I found that I got to like these Runyonesque people. People, what's more, whom in the normal run of life I would never have got to know, like drivers, builders, cleaners, porters, odd-job men; bookies, hustlers, gamblers big and small; con men and small-time crooks; students and pensioners, all sorts.

At poker, there is a particular companionship at the

table, much less than friendship but far more than casual acquaintance. It comes, this form of comradeship, from a shared interest and is not confined to poker. It occurs in any group with a common interest, be it horse players or stockbrokers. But it seems especially strong in poker, perhaps because players spend so much time together. And of course they are dealing with money, which touches everyone to the quick.

At the Vic, where I have formed the habit of dropping in almost every night when Suzy is away in Paris, I stick to the low stakes games. I am not even tempted by the big game. The satisfaction of (possibly) winning ten or twenty thousand would in any case be far outweighed by the gloom of taking a big hit.

Apart from the pleasure of playing itself, I seem to have all manner of unexpected, sometimes quite intimate, encounters. "How's your luck?" I usually greet people – not such a great question because it invariably produces a stream of bad beat stories. Ivan, for example, coming in at the top of the stairs saying, "Terrible lyuck, terrible lyuck!" in a thick Russian accent. "I got beaten by a full house. I had a house in five against aces-up. I got him all in, and on the end he hit an ace! Then I had trips against a four flush, I hit a full house and the other man made a straight flush! Now I just had aces-up and some idiot played on two 4s and made trips!"

"Ohmigod!" I tell him, "What a start to the month."

"Tyerrible!"

"But don't look at it just for tonight," I console him. "Take it over the whole year. Ninety-nine times out of a hundred you're going to win on these hands." He is obviously on his way to raise more money from a cash machine. "Don't play any more tonight, Ivan. Give it a miss."

Later, back at the table, he loses his new stake and jumps up to speak to me. "Cyan I give you a chyeque, please David?"

"No!"

Over at the big game there has been a row. Reg, who is a typical cockney low lifer, explains sibilantly: "This Ay-rab geezer, 'e's pouring it on, got five grand in front of 'im. Irish Pat, 'e's winning about six or seven. Then the Arab says, 'If I put up another £5,000, will you match it?' Pat says 'OK'. Pulls up the money.

"Along comes an Omaha hand, the flop is 10–8–5. Pat bets, the Ay-rab raises, Pat calls. Then comes another 5. The Arab says to Pat, 'Let's gamble!' He's been doing this, gamblin' like that all night.

"Now Pat don't like it. Starts to protest, 'What do you mean, "Let's gamble?" You're not supposed to speak durin' the 'and!' Calls over the floor manager, George, who 'asn't got a clue what's goin' on. George, 'e rules the bet can't go.

"Pat shows down a full 'ouse 5s on 10s and wins it, but 'e wouldn't 'ave dared call the Ay-rab if his five grand had gone in. The geezer could've 'ad a full house 10s or 8s. Everyone was disgusted with Pat and the game broke up right there."

Reg drew breath. "These big punters – they're all piss 'n wind, innit?"

I sit down with Leah, to talk about her appearing on a TV programme about women and poker which I am working on. She tells me, in a sudden intense rush:

"My mother died eleven days after I was born. Her

sister was forced to marry my father. She had to do it. My grandmother made her do it. It was the Jewish tradition, if your mother dies, the man marries her sister. She was always my mother to me, and I loved her as my mother, although she was not my real blood mother. She had a very unhappy life. A miserable life. I want women to lead their own lives.

"I only want to go on TV if I can show how women can lead their own lives and break down barriers!"

"I believe you can say that on TV," I tell Leah. "You've already set an example yourself."

She frowns. "Maybe."

And then Ibrahim, who is Iranian, a very talkative, enthusiastic, almost childish fellow, bounds up to me. This is a surreal moment.

"David! I want to ask you something."

"Sure, go ahead."

"It's about my son, yes? I want to have him circumcised. What do you think?"

"How old is he?"

"Seven."

"Well, Ibrahim, why now? It's a big decision."

"It's the custom, it's proper. But he never had it done. Do you know if it can be done?"

"It's got to be done as a medical operation at his age, Ibrahim, not a religious ritual."

"Can you tell me a good doctor?"

Next time I saw Ibrahim, I gave him the name of a Harley Street surgeon, not a *mohol.* Perhaps fortunately for his son, Ibrahim has not, as yet, booked the operation.

In case I have given too rosy a view of the Vic, here is another take on it. For weeks and months when he was seventeen, my youngest son Samson was longing to play at the Vic. He had a passion, back then, for poker and played with his chums at school and also occasionally in a light-hearted little game organised by Annie Griffin, producer of the TV film about women and gambling in which I played a part. Samson played like any seventeen-year-old, with great enthusiasm and no real judgement, but so what – it was great fun. He was longing for the day when he turned eighteen and would be legally old enough to join the Vic.

So on his birthday, we went out to dinner to his favourite restaurant and I drove over to the Edgware Road to enrol him as a 'member', as the rules of British casinos require. We went upstairs to the card room. A lot of people greeted me and looked at Sam as we walked around the tables, and then we left.

"So what did you think of it?" I inquired.

"Awful. Horrible. Sleazy to a degree."

"Wha-a-a-t?" I was astonished.

"Did you see how their eyes lit up when I came in with you? They saw the chance of doing up a new player! What a ghastly bunch!"

"They're OK," I protested feebly. "They're just club players, you know."

Sam shuddered. His enthusiasm for playing club poker took a sudden nosedive right off the graph. He still plays occasionally with school friends, but to this date, Sam has never set foot in the Vic, and it doesn't look as if he ever will.

The Man I Might Have Been

I first met Ernest in some poker game or other in London when he was about twenty-one or twenty-two years old, a fresh-looking lad from Yorkshire, with a round white face and round spectacles to go with it. He was obviously a useful player, but I didn't mark him down as anything special. He spoke with a fairly broad Yorkshire accent which made him seem a touch vulnerable, new to London. I was about twenty years older than Ernie, so I probably assumed a slightly patronising know-it-all manner.

We became friendly. Looking back, I suppose our friendship must always have had a father-son undercurrent to it. I knew more and had been around more – back in those days. Ernie learned slowly – he was a methodical, analytical chap – but he learned well.

Our friendship grew, we used to have dinner in the restaurant at the Vic or some other poker club and then play a bit. Ernie was a slow, controlled sort of player who evidently knew what he was doing. I remember going out to a little private game in Hendon, outside the law, where he seemed to clean up, playing Hold 'em, while I seemed to lose all the big hands. I still didn't reckon him much as a player, though. After all I had been educated at Cambridge and now worked for *The Times*. Ernie had come down from Barnsley Grammar 'oop north'.

Anyway, whenever Ernie was in London we met. As I have said, I like poker conversations, going over old hands, recalling bad beats, how you should have played it, and so on. Ernie rapidly became (I had to admit) more knowledgeable than me. He liked good cooking, got to know wine, had a certain assurance about him, while retaining his style as a Yorkshire lad. We went to Crockford's and most of the Park Lane casinos. I never invited him to our regular Tuesday night game. I was afraid he would not fit in, he was by now too much of an expert, an apprentice professional. He once told me (referring to my own expulsion from the game) that if he had played, he would have played so fast and loose he would never have been remotely in danger of being banned – and of course taken down the money in the process.

One impression which got to me was Ernie's paranoia, so I thought, about cards. If he lost, as of course happened sometimes, and in particular at a certain little card club in north London, Ernie was convinced it was because of cheating. There was collusion or marking of cards. It was not his certainty that he was a better player, as he probably was, which led to this conclusion. It was based on observation, of little things which happened at the table which he picked up on, which he claimed were not right.

I used to pooh-pooh Ernie's suspicions as imaginary, but he became quite famous for the strength of his views, and didn't mind who heard them. No doubt there was *some* cheating in these sort of places. One could never be absolutely sure. Ernie was.

Eventually, after he got a taste for Las Vegas, he gave up playing in London altogether. He also suspected cheating over there from time to time, and again, didn't mind voicing his suspicions. In one long-running spat, he offered to put up $25,000, to be held by the Horseshoe casino in Vegas, to persuade a particular player he was accusing to undergo a lie detector test. If he failed to pass the test, Ernie would collect the $25,000 surety the man had to put up on his side. It was a generous offer, in Ernie's view, because he himself could not win – the man would only take the test if he could pass it. The challenge was not accepted.

Later on Ernie drew a distinction between what he termed 'hard' cheating in London and 'soft' cheating in Vegas. In London, so he felt, there might be serious collusion between a player and a dealer, by holding out cards or tampering with the deck away from the table, so as to 'cold deck' a game. In America, as he saw it, the danger was less. Two pros might help each other, worn or old cards might get marked. But there could not, by definition, be serious cheating because if there had been he could never have won. After all, there are cameras on every table and a lot of knowledgeable people around.

Blackjack also came to figure in his life. Ernie was a competent player. He could beat the single deck games in Vegas and elsewhere with a simple staking strategy of one to two. He wanted to play in London and devised a little ruse, a joke really, to conceal his expertise. After dinner at a plush Mayfair casino, I was deputed to bet it up at the roulette table as a decoy, while Ernie bet serious money at blackjack.

What happened in practice was that after wining and dining in wild extravagance, courtesy of the casino, we would make a detour by the gaming salon. Ernie's desire to gamble then took over. Scattering his chips across the lay-out like confetti, any edge he might have at blackjack was lost to the wind. Strangely enough I wasn't much good at this, gingerly placing four or five chips here and there, while Ernie ordered me to plonk it on in lumps. I doubt if the management watching us so closely was taken in –

more likely put me down as the kind of rich twit often found dropping his money in Mayfair casinos.

Ernie got into several scrapes in Vegas as a result of his success at blackjack. Pit bosses hate players whom they think are counting and mostly don't understand the way they work. In a most celebrated case (which I slightly mis-reported in my book *Inside the Gambler's Mind*) Ernie gave evidence on behalf of an English friend, after the security people had accused him of cheating. Ernie had left the game before this incident but his friend had been marched out to the 'back room', a frightening experience from the bad old days.

In court, the casino's lawyer thought he was going to turn Ernie, this callow-looking young English fellow, inside out. He put a series of seemingly innocuous questions to him – Did he know any methods of cheating at blackjack? Ernie said he had heard people could crimp the picture cards or mark cards with their nails. Would it surprise him to know, the lawyer asked, that there were several other methods of cheating? Ernie replied it would not surprise him. As a poker player, he was well aware that the lawyer was setting a trap for him. Then it came:

"Is it possible that your friend was cheating, and that you were unaware of it?"

Ernie was not going to answer any question beginning "Is it possible . . . ?" He had donned his best Yorkshire suit and tie for his court appearance. Drawing himself up like an envoy presenting his letters of appointment to the Queen, he turned to the judge. "Your Honour, I'm really awf'lly sorry, but I simply don't understand the question."

The judge, practically creasing himself in laughter, told the smart-ass lawyer to stand the witness down. This was not a question about what Ernie as a witness had seen or not seen, it was entirely hypothetical.

Ernie's friend, the defendant, who was a persistent and pugnacious fellow, then sued the casino for damages. He was awarded $48,000, plus interest on his confiscated winnings.

In another incident, at a little casino out in the desert, Ernie was not so lucky. His substantial blackjack winnings were withheld, and it took a long rearguard action to get the decision reversed. But in the nature of things, casinos can delay and prevaricate, and I don't think he ever got all the money back.

In a memorable act of revenge, a real *coup de théâtre*, Ernie took them on at craps. At one moment there was a mass of players crowding round the dice table, betting in fives and tens. And then there was Ernie betting in hundreds. As if by magic a space opened up for him. He bet on the front line, on come bets, on hard-ways, on numbers, he pressed and pressed again, betting up a storm. In about ten or fifteen minutes he ran up over $40,000, tipped the crew and quit. After that, as is the nature of casinos, they couldn't do enough for Ernie and his party, which included a young woman he was toting around as a cover at the blackjack tables. Everything was 'comped' – provided as a complimentary service.

Later I discovered Ernie's success with dice was double-edged. Like so many poker professionals who wager madly on sports bets or golf, he had a 'leak'. Dice was his. Why card players who are so brilliant in their calculation at poker choose to splurge all their money on a mindless gamble at dice or other casino games is hard to explain. "I just like craps," was all Ernie would ever say, but his losses, when he was caught up in a serious bout of craps were, I know, horrendous. I suppose poker players figure they can always get it back at the card table.

And Ernie did. During his 20s and his 30s, he became a man of property. He bought a house in Yorkshire and paid off his parents' mortgage – no matter how long he was away following the poker trail, Ernie always stayed very close to his family. What they made of his chosen career is another matter – until he was aged thirty his mother continued to mail him advertisements for 'respectable' jobs like banking. His father had run vending machines for soft drinks and cigarettes. Ernie bought a little house in the suburbs of Las Vegas and rented an apartment in Los Angeles, after the poker action moved over there. He also acquired a holiday home in the south-west of France. He must have won plenty when the going was good.

Yet so often he seemed miserable, at his losing runs. This is the point about the professional life which put me off (assuming I had the talent for it, which I hadn't). Watching Ernie play, I hardly ever saw him fail to win a hand. He would drop ten or twenty thousand at the seven card stud game at the Mirage and then we would go off to dinner somewhere. Ernie knew all the restaurants and, surprisingly for Vegas, there were some good ones. He affected to be cheerful, but still . . . "What I want," he would lament, "is to find a nice girl and settle down. And win a few pots for a change."

Ernie's misery seemed to be like a garment which slipped over his psyche. He was considering mortgaging his house, or borrowing from other players. I didn't inquire about his finances too closely. I would see Ernie only once a year at the World Series, or occasionally in London, and it was always the same story. Broke! I suspected that Ernie played one level higher than he ought to have done. Granted he was a top player, but there were other top players around competing against him.

In reality, Ernie had very sensibly tied up his money, he was only cash broke. He followed what he called the 'box theory'. When the game stops and the guys go home to sleep, they leave their bankroll, in cash or chips, in a box in the casino safe deposit, ready for the next game. "No matter how much I have in my box," Ernie explained laconically, "I know I'll find a way of losing it." It could be at dice, or playing too high, or simply playing badly. He might play well night after night and then have a couple of bad nights which would wipe out all his profits.

It was to counter this self-destructive urge that Ernie invested in property, deliberately making it as difficult as possible to get his hands on his own money. A lot of players who failed to take this sort of precaution and then gambled all the money in their boxes were, literally, broke. Ernie was never broke in that sense, but his cash flow, when he had a losing run, might dry up, so he had to borrow to get back in the game.

As he approached forty, Ernie felt gloomy about his life. "There's nowhere to go from here," was how he put it. "Nothing I can achieve with the knowledge I've got." Ernie meant that if you are a doctor you can become a surgeon. If you are a politician you may, one day, rise to be Prime Minister. Even a blackjack dealer could climb the ladder and turn into a highly paid executive.

Ernie felt, as a poker player, he had made the grade and he was right. Yet the only thing he could do was take a seat in the big game and he had been there, done that. There was nowhere further to go. "All the knowledge

I have gained," Ernie complained, "is useless!" No casino would ever employ him and the people they did employ knew a lot less, in fact, than he did. Poker players are not supposed to have existential doubts. Nothing I could say about his achievements could shake this mood.

Ernie was always protesting he was looking for a girl to settle down with. But when would he get the time to find her? At one stage my hopes rose – he acquired a regular girlfriend who was very Californian, sharp, funny and pretty. She was a blackjack dealer herself, so she understood the gamblin' life. They had some good times and Ernie visited her family but it came to nowt. He must have realized that poker is terribly hard for a woman. Unless she's a player herself, a woman either sits behind her husband's chair, as Mrs. Johnny Moss did for years on end, watching the cards go by, or she is on her own. Not much of a life.

In that context, I remember Ernie sitting behind my chair once, when I was playing a low-level game of Omaha and coaching me – *"Bet it! Raise it! Raise him back!"* – with a whisper in my ear. Sure enough I began to rack up all the chips I had lost (I was the miserable one then) in the previous session. As he could obviously beat this sort of game out of sight, why didn't he play these games himself, instead of the big games? I asked. "Can't make enough to support my lifestyle," he explained. "Couple of thousand a month is no use at all."

It cost Ernie $32 an hour to play in the high stakes game in the California cardrooms. If he played say, 35 hours a week, plus tips, that is close to $1,200. At the weekends, it cost about $170 to fly back to Vegas, and $100 to rent a car. The apartment in L.A. was $1,600 a month. He ate out seven nights a week. So one way or another he had to win about $12,000 a month just to break even. And with table money at this level, you had to be a pretty good player just to break even in these games. Over six months, he might make $60,000 net profit and then suffer a losing run which would put him back to square one.

Still, Ernie had his freedom. There was no alarm clock in his life and in the summer he regularly took a three-month break. Better than working? I would say more or less the same as working, without the assurance of a regular salary cheque or the consolation of a pension at the end of it all. Maybe if I was young and single and had no family to look after, I might try it – maybe.

Ernie also had his successes, including winning a World Series title, which is the ultimate accolade. It happened in the seven card high-low split event. First prize was $94,000. "I'm very surprised," Ernie was quoted in the press report, adding with characteristic Yorkshire phlegm: "I'm delighted that I finally got back some of the money I've poured into these tournaments over the years."

As I wrote at the time, Ernie showed true grit. He was down to his last seven chips before the dinner break, which allowed him just two more antes. His first hand when he resumed play was no good, of the K-10-6 variety, but then he was dealt a playable hand, which picked up the antes. In two more hands he had moved from zero to $18,000 in chips, and was ready to battle his way through to the final table. When it came down to the last two, Ernie got lucky, so he modestly explained, by outdrawing a better player than himself. So against all expectations a couple of hours earlier, he found himself snapping a tournament winner's gold bracelet round his wrist.

Then one day, Ernie confided he had found the right girl. She was a Vietnamese-American, a graduate in business studies, quiet, but well read and an affectionate companion. So it *was* possible to settle down and lead a normal life on the pro circuit in Vegas.

I looked forward to hearing of Ernie's wedding. Alas, the romance evaporated in the shimmering air of the Nevada desert. It was not poker which got between them. She never went to a casino to watch him play. Ernie prided himself on getting back home every night at seven p.m., just like a guy in a regular job, so they could go out to dinner together. He visited her family and she flew over and went up to Yorkshire a couple of times to meet his folks. He didn't really know what went wrong. Perhaps she just wanted to find someone closer to her own age. Ernie was very upset. Not surprisingly, he blew a lot of money.

Ernie's coming through all those years of hard grind, of winning and losing and starting over again made me wonder if, perhaps, I could have survived in the poker life. If I could have been like Ernie, instead of becoming a journalist, if the cards had fallen that way. It *is* an amusing life, there *are* a lot of good friends around. Ernie has made it. But, as the old saying has it, "You play the hand you're dealt."

I think I got lucky.

2

Gambling, joy of

The action is everything, more consuming than sex, more immediate than politics; more important always than the acquisition of money, which is never, for the gambler, the true point of the exercize.

Joan Didion, *The White Album*

What if you met a man in a bar this evening, after you quit work for the day, and he said (as people sometimes do), "Hey, let's toss a coin for a pound, heads or tails."

"Right here in front of everybody?"

"Why not!"

"Okay," you might say, if you were in that sort of mood. "Let's go for it!"

But then the man adds: "Just one little thing about this toss I want to explain before we start. When I win, you lose your pound. When you win, I'll pay you only 99 pence."

It's not all that different, is it, one penny on the toss? But you would be out of your mind to take on such a proposition, wouldn't you? Especially if your spouse or, worse, your employer, happened to be watching. You would be marked down as an idiot if you couldn't handle your money any better. A pound to 99 pence. Why do it? It makes no sense.

But that is exactly what all of us do when we gamble, when we cross the threshold between workaday life and the fantasy realm of a casino. In fact, if the house gets only one per cent of an edge or advantage, gamblers consider it a good bet. If they can get even money, one for one on their stake (as in certain bets at dice), they think it's great value.

I have a confession to make, right at the start. I am not a gambler. Not any more, that is. I have learned the hard way, as most of us do, that you cannot beat the laws of probability.

On my first visit to Las Vegas, as a freshman on vacation from Cambridge University, I came prepared with a system for roulette. My idea was to wait for a series of reds or blacks to come up, six in a row, and then start betting on the other colour, doubling up after each losing spin until I hit a winner. So after six reds, say, I would start betting black: $1, then $2, $4, $8, $16, $32, $64, $128. For the system to lose, the same colour would have to come up 15 times in a row, which seemed highly unlikely. My only anxiety, as I recall, was that the initial run of six consecutive reds or blacks would take such a long time to appear that I might get bored waiting.

I need not have worried. After a couple of hours logging the wheel, I was ready to launch my system. The first spin went down, the next spin went down, and the next, and the next, with terrifying speed, as red kept repeating. Suddenly, like a flash of light striking the brow of a philosopher, the realization penetrated my fevered intent. This particular roulette wheel did not give a damn about me and my pathetic hopes of fortune. It was oblivious to the fact that I had travelled 7,000 miles across an ocean and most of a continent to test my luck. If I was to follow my system, I had to bet $256 on the next spin. I also had six weeks of summer vacation to pay for. The croupier was eyeing my precarious tower of chips like an explosives expert about to dynamite a building. I pulled back – just in time.

Nearly everyone makes this mistake in gambling, which is to confuse the short-term outcome with long-term probability. On every individual spin, the probability of red or black is the same, 50:50. And over a million spins, reds and blacks will virtually even out (ignoring zeros). But within that series, there will be many short-term fluctuations on either side. Fourteen reds in a row is no big deal.

It is good to learn this lesson young. When I go to Las Vegas now, I don't even *see* the slot machines. I feel almost guilty – considering the immense and multifarious efforts the casinos make to tempt the visitor to gamble – that I do not spend a dime on casino games. My passion lies elsewhere. I play poker, a game of skill, albeit with a big gambling element in it. What I like is the ambience of gambling, particularly casino gambling, with its day-into-night and night-into-day sense of anything-goes-and-here-it-comes release from the conventions of ordinary life.

Everyone takes chances, every day, although people do not consciously classify the process as gambling. Every time you drive, every time you buckle up in an airplane seat, one might say every time you cross the road, the risk is there. These are unavoidable risks in the modern world and for most people, so habitual as not to be worth worrying about. *Che sarà sarà*. These days, there is danger in riding the subway, danger in visiting New York's World Trade Centre, danger even in visiting a government building in Oklahoma City, let alone in travelling abroad.

Other sorts of risks, such as those inherent in active sports like skiing, mountaineering, horseback riding, sailing, even golf, are more easily avoided. The pleasure of doing it is what gets people involved. That pleasure far outweighs any vestigial concern about something going wrong. Besides, regardless of the sport, everyone involved has had a least a degree of initial training to prepare himself or herself and to guard against accidents. The odds of coming through safely are tilted well in your favour.

Even in matters of investment, such as taking out a life insurance policy, which means, in effect, betting on your own longevity, the gamble is a studied risk, founded on actuarial tables and the prudent desire to protect your family. The insurance company, working on the past record of hundreds of thousands of instances, calculates the probability of a particular misfortune befalling the applicant, and sets its premium accordingly, adding a healthy margin to cover operating costs and allow for a profit.

The insurance companies are not really gambling themselves, because they are operating on the basis of statistics that virtually guarantee them a positive return. Yes, but then we remember Lloyd's of London. Even the best regulated risks sometimes come unstuck. I think it was James Thurber who observed: "There is no safety in numbers; there is no safety anywhere."

Casino gambling is risk taking in its purest form. The participants willingly and deliberately get involved, knowing the chances are not in their favour. No one has to do it. All players are aware that the odds are against them. The odds are set out in all the books, even in government reports on gambling. The question is: why do people still do it?

It may seem a paradox to insist that money is not what gambling is about. Of course, money is the essence of gambling and the way you keep score. Games of chance without money involved simply do not work. And you cannot gamble in a casino without money. Money is the fuel of gambling; it drives it, as petrol powers a car, but the pleasure of driving a car is not about petroleum. It's about speed, style, movement. Fuel is merely what makes the car run. In that sense, the real motives behind gambling are to be sought elsewhere.

Play, the enjoyment of play, is a part of human nature. It is an instinct as old as the sex drive, as powerful as hunger and thirst, as basic to the human condition as survival. Gambling is a heightened form of play. That is why so many people like gambling, and spend so much money on it, not just all over Britain and the United States now that the brakes are off, but in virtually all societies in the modern world.

The appeal of gambling, to my mind, is in the action. The phrase 'where the action is' derives from Damon Runyon's story, 'The Idyll of Miss Sarah Brown' (1947), which celebrates the exploits of gambler Sky Masterson. The immortal Sky Masterson got his name, you remember, because he liked to bet so high, on any proposition whatever, that he would bet all he had. "The Sky is strictly a player . . . As far as The Sky is concerned, money is just something for him to play with and the dollars may as well be doughnuts as far as value goes with him."

Action expresses, in a word, the whole gambling experience. It means playing with chance, taking a challenge, the excitement of living in top gear. In gambling, this is the pay-off. In our routine urban lives, most of us are cogs in the wheel of work, taxes, social and family obligations. Gambling offers a fast way out. On the green baize, or at the track, or at a lottery terminal the player can give self-indulgence a whirl, briefly cast responsibility aside, and fantasize about a brighter, richer, easier life. It is not, in reality, going to work out like that. But some people do win, don't they? In lotteries, almost unimaginable sums of money.

Here it is useful to distinguish different forms of gambling by the pay offs they offer: long range versus short-term; degrees of social gratification; profit and loss. Each kind of gamble offers its own appeal.

First, the long range gamble, as in lotteries. In terms of odds, of many millions to one against winning, lotteries are a bad gamble. Their appeal, which certainly elicits a deep response across a huge swathe of the population, lies in the prospect of acquiring superstar wealth, as if the finger of fate were suddenly to reach out and touch one lucky person. All of this can be purchased for a very small price. For a period before the draw – it may be just a few minutes, or may last for days – people can daydream about what they would do with the money. And why not? It is a harmless enough little dream, which can lighten dull lives. Lottery players know that only one winner will make it big. What their purchase of a ticket gives them is a little spoonful of hope, which, like honey, is pleasing while it lasts.

Experience shows that lotteries tend to exploit low income sectors of the population. Besides being least able to afford this kind of spending, which is of course an indirect form of taxation, such people tend to be most vulnerable to the lottery promoters' blandishments. Indeed, what may be most troubling about lotteries in America is slogans like "Your way out of the ghetto" and other enticements used by state agencies to attract bettors.

A great deal of gambling, at the popular level, is geared to a short-term, almost instantaneous, thrill. This is what casinos offer. Unlike lotteries, the odds seem within reach. Casino gamblers look down on lotteries because the odds are too long to offer a practical expectation of gain, whereas slot machines, dice, blackjack and roulette can provide an immediate return. At a fast-moving game of roulette, there may be up to 75 coups an hour. A slot machine, without the intermediary of a dealer or croupier, or any need for know-how on the part of the player, offers perhaps five or six coups per minute. With a slot machine, the thrill of the action as the gambler inserts the coins, pulls the handle, or presses the buttons, is almost continuous – as long as the money lasts. American gamblers have become so enamoured of slots that they now account for about 65 per cent of casino gambling.

It should be noted, in passing, that there is no skill involved in casino games (with the single exception of blackjack, and some of the poker slot machines). What gamblers get is speed and intensity of action, plus the chance of hitting a winning streak that can lead to a big win, the win that will salve all their previous losses. At roulette, the queen of casino games, hitting the right number pays 35 to 1. Never mind that the edge against the player on the double-zero game is an iniquitous 5.26 per cent, compared with only 2.7 per cent on the single-zero British game. If luck, i.e. short-term fluctuation, runs your way, you can break the bank or at least win a small fortune. (What is the sure-fire way to make a small fortune in a casino? Answer, start out with a large fortune.)

The gambling games offered by casinos act like a drug. It's part physical and part psychological; highs and lows, over and over, in rapid succession. These fluctuations of loss and gain, the glint of light and clink of action, awareness of other people gambling, the sense underneath it all of playing with risk, of living on the edge of danger, are exciting. This is what the expression 'getting the adrenaline going' means. The physical sensation – dryness in the throat, sweaty palms, butterflies in the stomach, the feeling of every nerve on full alert – is, for many people, highly pleasurable.

Some psychologists have suggested a parallel between gambling and sexual excitement: build-up, climax, release of tension, repeated over and over. There is no need to push the analogy too far to make the point that gambling carries a strong emotional charge.

To increase the sense of indulgence, of fantasy, of losing hold of reality, casinos create an ambience far removed from the surroundings of ordinary life. No clocks. No daylight. Seductive lighting. Flashes of surreal colour. The whir of the slots. The beat of music, pulsing under the noise of greeting, shouts, ringing jackpots and whoops from winners. Drinks on the house – "Keep 'em coming, baby!" – and on every side, the half-open sexual turn-on of cutey-pie dealers in miniskirts or cowboy gear. What a heady, glamorous mix! How can anyone long resist it?

All of it is designed to disorient the gamblers and keep them playing. The whole operation driven – this is most important – by easy credit. "Another two thousand, Mr. Ashuro? Just sign this slip, sir."

The social component of gambling, varying from game to game, finds its most extreme expression in baccarat. The baccarat pit is usually separated from the casino floor by a rail; bystanders can admire or envy it only at a distance. The excitement of baccarat comes from the sheer size of the stakes, up to $250,000 a hand in the case of Australian tycoon Kerry Packer and a few other very rich men.

Again, it is a game requiring no skill whatsoever. (Two sides, Bank and Player, each draw two cards with the option of a third card, to see who gets closer to a total of nine). Baccarat caters to a select group of monied players who probably can afford more or less anything they want in material terms but who relish the challenge of high stakes play, of taking on the house, 'to confront their destiny', as some of the oriental high rollers put it. The players know that each hand is the equivalent of, say, the price of a sports car, but the bets are treated simply as so many plastic chips.

What gives this kind of gambling its cachet, its style, is not just the high stakes but another dimension of the game, which might be termed 'social pampering'. Baccarat provides a handful of top casinos – there is a pecking order among casinos as well – with the cream of their revenue. In America, the managers of these casinos will do anything and everything to attract the high rollers: not merely the routine 'comps' (complimentary services) of a free flight and private suite accorded all big gamblers, but the kind of personal attention (such as a favourite chef on call 24 hours a day) designed to gratify a particular customer's every whim. Such high pampering is not readily obtainable in ordinary life, even to the rich. (Girls? Perish the thought! Las Vegas casino managers claim they would never risk their gaming licences for petty prostitution. Frankly, Dave, I'm surprised you even asked!)

Casino staffs include a particular category of employee called a 'host' whose role is to take care of high rollers. The host and the guest each understand that their relationship, cordial as it may be, is based on a false premise – namely the narrow 1.2 per cent house edge on baccarat which, cumulatively, is immensely profitable to the casino. But both sides conspire to accept the relationship at face value. Sometimes the players win a million or two (but so long as they keep coming back, the casino isn't worried).

The social aspect of gambling comes out most clearly in horse racing. The race track offers a quite different kind of gamble from casino play. For one thing, racing has a public image: people attend race tracks in large numbers, and they read about racing in the papers. The sport can be enjoyed for its own sake. Racing brings together a wide-ranging fraternity of owners, trainers, jockeys, and other followers whose common link is their enthusiasm for the game. In England, this identity of interest runs from the Queen herself all the way down to the cloth-capped punter in the betting shop.

More significantly, from the gambling point of view, horse racing (unlike most casino games) allows room for judgement. The bettor has lots of information to weigh: all the variables of running, timing, handicapping and so on that comprise form. Punters are notably studious, and the intervals set between races allow time to resolve the more or less insoluble equation of form, to pick a winner. This is a relatively measured form of betting, but being available almost every day, it still carries as much risk of becoming compulsive as any other form of gambling. It is satisfying to make your own judgement (especially if it proves right), but racing is still a gamble – much more so than games such as bridge or backgammon, in which a player's skill, in the shape of his or her own decisions, determines the result.

The element of skill finds its most complete expression in professional gambling. As the odds in gambling are, by definition, against the player, 'professional gambling' is something of a misnomer. It connotes players who have managed to turn the odds in their favour. The only casino game in which this occurs is blackjack. Thanks to mathematician Edward Thorp's landmark book *Beat the Dealer*, reprinted many times since it took the gambling world by storm in the 1960s, many thousands of players have learned 'counting' (a way of keeping track of the cards in order to increase the stakes when the outcome appears favourable). Casinos abhor counters, don't really understand them, and do their utmost to detect and bar them.

In casinos, the only professionals (blackjack counters are an endangered species) are poker players. By 'professional' I mean they expect to win more than they lose and follow no other occupation. Their edge comes from exploiting the weakness of less skilled players. "Ain't only three things to gamblin'," according to W.C. 'Puggy' Pearson, a former world poker champion. "Knowin' the 60:40 end of a proposition, money management, and knowin' yourself." There is at the same time a camaraderie among groups of gamblers, whether they are card players, horse race punters or stock market speculators, which gives their activity the extra dimension of a sense of belonging, beyond the activity itself.

'On the turf and under it,' as they say in horse racing, 'all men are equal.' The same goes for the green baize of the poker table. No one cares at poker who you are, or where you come from, or even what you look like. The only thing that counts is how you play. I particularly like the expression 'cards speak' – especially as I come from England, where your accent immediately defines your social status. 'Cards speak' means that when the hands are shown down, the ranking of the cards decides the outcome – even if a player miscalls his hand as sometimes happens.

The *equality* of poker, which is the virtue of the game, is usually taken for granted. It means that any player can sit down with any other player – duke or dustman, millionaire or shoe clerk – on the same terms. All the other differences which grade and regulate social distinctions in everyday life disappear. A new player has only to put up the ante: there is no 'glass ceiling' holding anyone back. You can play alongside a world champion, which would be out of the question in other sports, like golf or tennis. Hard to imagine driving off the tee with Tiger Woods or returning service from Sampras, or facing Kasparov across the chess board, on equal terms.

What's more, in poker the reverse situation also holds true. An amateur as rich and celebrated as Bill Gates can be quite happy, as has happened, to sit down in the $3–$6 game at the Mirage and play with the locals. The chances are the same for everyone. Obviously the money meant nothing to Mr. Gates.

Two of the top pros, Doyle Brunson and Chip Reese, were playing $300–$600 limit at a nearby table. According to a report on the net, they invited Gates to join their game. He didn't want to do so but asked Brunson to sign a copy of his poker book *Super/System*. Brunson said if Gates didn't want to play, he wasn't going to autograph his book for him. Someone else commented on the net that even if Gates got on a rush and won everybody's money, winning in the big game would still be meaningless to him financially. Maybe he thought the baby game was more amusing.

In fact, high stakes players will often play *down*, so as to take a shot at lower-level opponents. The pros' motive, of course, is to win their money. But the amateurs get the opportunity (if they so choose) to compete with the best. Maybe they will learn something – even if they have to pay for the privilege. "Lessons are extra", as Edward G. Robinson observed in his classic put-down in the movie *The Cincinatti Kid*.

At the table it is *how* everyone plays that counts. The same kind of easy relationship applies to musicians, who do not even have to speak each other's language. The only criterion in a jam session is how they play. A common language obviously helps: conversations take place at the poker table which players might never venture in 'real life'. Some of the talk is very personal – I am continually surprised how strangers will volunteer details of their love life or sensitive issues like the illness of a child.

Part of this chat, which everyone indulges in, is calculated, as players try to read each other's style and smoke each other out. All the same, the social dimension of poker gives it a warmth and value notably absent from other forms of gambling. Such familiarity cuts especially deep in a regular poker school where the players get to know each other inside out, over a period of years. It is a curious relationship: typically, the players have far more than a casual acquaintance with each other and yet far less than true friendship.

The same goes for horse racing. "The race book is open seven days a week, three hundred and sixty-five days a year," noted John Rosecrance in his amusing and informative study *The Degenerates of Lake Tahoe* (published by Peter Lang). "Individual gamblers know, with certainty, that various group members will be available on a daily basis . . . The relationships that have developed between inveterates can be considered a form of comradeship."

Comrade is given in the dictionary as: "A person who has interests or concerns in common with others and shares in their activities," as distinct from *friend*: "A person whom one knows well and is fond of," notes Rosecrance.

Comrades remain comrades only at the poker table. If a player is away for a while, the relationship cuts out. As one horse player explained: "When you're here, you're important. When you're gone, you're just gone." You may be 'fond of' another player (male or female) but that is outside the game itself – where the individuals are competing (or should be) as rivals.

This points up an intriguing aspect of poker, which is how to draw the line between 'work' and 'play'. If you play too much it becomes 'work'. Yet people regard this work as 'play'. It is a bit too simple to say that professionals play for money and the rest of us for fun. In my observation, professionals also play for 'fun', because they like playing better than just about anything else they know.

Because *money* is how you keep score at gambling games – rather than points or runs or goals – the outcome is significant to each player in an immediate, personal way. At one extreme it may mean a player can't afford a taxi after the game. (Haven't we all suffered this indignity in our younger days?) At the other extreme, in the euphoria of a big win, a player might go out and splurge his winnings on a sports car, or a diamond necklace for a girlfriend, or some other extravagance. That's why there are so many shopping malls in casinos. The only trouble is that after spending these winnings, who knows when the next losing run may strike?

Very many people who like to think of themselves as playing for money, to make a living or supplement their jobs, are fooling themselves. Look at all those *habitués* of card rooms in Vegas and the poker palaces of Los Angeles – lonely divorcees and retirees scrabbling to supplement their pensions, vacationers trying to pay for their trip to the bright lights, dealers on a break (if they were strong players, why would they ever take a job dealing?).

Such players may not all be losers, granted, but they are sure as hell not winners in the sense of making a livelihood from the game. They are, at best, break-even players. Even many 'professionals' can be extremely unprofessional. Leaving aside the difficulty of being a consistent winner, most big money players appear to have what is known as 'a leak' – sloughing off money on sports bets or golf or other gambles. In such activities, they are more or less bound to be frequent if not habitual losers.

Top poker players, in my observation, often seem just as

broke as the amateurs, but at a higher level of broke-ness. If they were consistent winners, why would so many pros need to borrow money from each other all the time? If it is not sports bets, it must be that they go broke by overreaching their ambition at poker. The bad beat syndrome is as old as Adam and Eve. (It was all the serpent's fault!)

So who winds up with the money? It is a mistake to see poker as a zero-sum game, in which the money lost by the losers goes to the winners in a perfectly balanced transfer. There is a third element in the transaction – the house! The house takes its cut from each hand or on each hour. Is there any question, at the end of the session or the end of the year, who the big winner is? The Bellagio's annual win from poker is probably $25m.–$30m.

Pros who make a good living from poker expect to pay tax on their earnings like other citizens in regular jobs. (I have heard world champions groan about the high rate of their tax just like a typical businessman.) They probably 'work' longer hours than their accountants. So why do so many people go on playing when most of them are losing or only breaking even? We come back to the action. "If I'm not in action, I've got nothing," an astute gambler once noted. "If I'm in action, anything is possible." The card room (like the race book) is the place to go, to share a common passion. It's where the present-day counterparts of Sky Masterson hang out.

The truly professional gamblers are the casinos themselves. "If you wanna make money in a casino, own one!" advises Steve Wynn, president of Mirage Resorts, Inc. As the most successful operator in the gaming industry, he has proved his point. The casinos, by gratifying the gambling instincts of the rest of us, are betting on a sure thing. The odds are always in their favour. And if they get the operation right (not as easy it looks, as competition gets tougher) they must win. It took Wall Street some time to grasp this basic truth and accept casino stocks as respectable. They are now a popular – perhaps even blue chip – investment.

The rise of legalised gambling has consequences that are double-edged for communities and individuals. The irony is that while the individual pleasures and psychic rewards of gambling have generally been under-appreciated, the social and economic benefits of legalised betting are generally overestimated.

It was Atlantic City that launched the gambling spree across the United States, taking it well beyond the arid confines of Nevada. The first casino opened its doors on the Boardwalk in 1978. Atlantic City became a model for other jurisdictions eager to cash in, so they fondly imagined, on easy money. It was an unfortunate model, because, as anyone who has been there can vouch, Atlantic City is a dismal failure. Instead of being transformed into a new community, the old resort has remained essentially what it was, a glorified dump. But one with gaming revenues greater than all the casinos on the Las Vegas strip.

There are exceptions to the Atlantic City model. The most extraordinary, surreal even, eruption of gambling in America has occurred in an unlikely location: the green hills of Connecticut. Foxwoods, on the 1,200 acre reservation of the Mashantucket Pequot tribe, is now the most successful casino in the United States, indeed, in the English-speaking world. It plays host to 40,000 visitors a day. Foxwoods' overall casino win (money held after paying out the winners before expenses) is estimated at well over $1 billion a year. And all this since February 1992.

So successful has Foxwoods been, that another Indian tribe was attracted to the area, the Mohegans. (The valediction to 'The last of the Mohicans' was premature – they not only survived but are now thriving.) The tribe set up its own casino, in partnership with Sol Kerzner of Sun City fame in South Africa without even denting, so it seems, Foxwoods' soaring enterprise. In 1998, Foxwoods and its Indian neighbour set a slots record of $1.114 billion. Foxwoods has also brought new employment to a region in decline. The collapse of the shipbuilding industry in New London as a result of post-Cold War military cutbacks cost 6,000 jobs. Foxwoods has more than made up this total and has plans to add still more hotels and entertainments.

The danger is that many of the jurisdictions that are so confidently promoting gambling today may discover that the economic benefits are illusory. Even Foxwoods could some day see an end to the endless torrent of money, as competition in the region rises. What tends to occur is a diversion, rather than a net growth of economic resources. Gambling is, after all, different from other leisure activities. It can hurt people, it can encourage false hopes and at its worst undermine whole sections of society.

Mississippi is one of those places where the economic benefits are substantial and accepted as such. New Orleans has proved a disappointment. Some commentators – and not just anti-gambling zealots and religious nuts – fear that if gambling is let rip, as seems to be happening in the United States, entire communities and not just individuals may suffer.

Certainly no one would deny that gambling needs to be prudently controlled. Controlled, in my view, not for the benefit of the casinos or the state, but in *the interests of the gamblers themselves.* They are the people who make it all happen but, typically, they are the last group to be considered by well-meaning or do-gooding legislators. A night at the casino or a day at the race track is a highly stimulating activity. But they do not occur in a social vacuum, like, say, tossing a coin.

Anyway, that is my view of gambling.[1] Everyone involved has their own ideas about it. Gambling, whether you agree or disagree, is an activity difficult to define, with multifarious off-shoots – economic, legal, social, psychological, sporting, mathematical and so on. Which is why the study of gambling and research into gambling has so proliferated in recent years. Outstanding in this development has been a series of international conferences on gambling held at regular two or three-year intervals for the past twenty years, designed to bring the assorted followers of the game together.

The first conference I attended was the sixth, held at Bally's pink hotel casino in Atlantic City, in December 1984. The next one was at Bally's even bigger pink casino in Reno, in July 1987. The conferences were fun, for two reasons. By day there were lectures and seminars on all aspects of gambling. By night, many of the delegates liked to hit the tables, especially (I noted) casino operators from faraway places like London. As if having been denied the

[1] Adapted from an article published in *Wilson's Quarterly*, January 1995

pleasure of gambling on their own turf, they could hardly wait to cut free on someone else's pitch.

The series of International Conferences on Gambling and Risk Taking were the inspiration of a professor of economics at the University of Nevada, Reno, Bill Eadington, the author of numerous papers on gambling and Director of the Institute for the Study of Gambling and Commercial Gaming at the university. He brought to these gatherings – which were subsequently held in Las Vegas, London and then Montreal, each one bigger than the last – a kind of understated enthusiasm and authority which made those who attended feel the event was special and worthwhile. (I am a bit biased because over the years the Eadington family and my family became close friends.)

I think I was usually the only journalist regularly present at these jamborees. Certainly reporting in the press was very sparse, which I think was remiss, given the importance of gambling in modern American life. In my experience in London, only two kinds of gambling story excite news editors. 1. 'Arab high rollers in betting coup.' 2. 'Call girls in casino scandal.' I suppose the ideal story would be 'Arab high rollers in call girl scandal' – guaranteed to hit the front page of every paper in town.

No such luck at the gambling conferences! Instead, a mass of learned papers would be read and debated, later to be published in a series of hefty volumes by the university. These books collate an immense amount of thought and knowledge about gambling, ranging from the gaming industry's strictly practical concerns at one end to theoretical research at the other. As such, they constitute a key source for the study of gambling in our time. I went to my first conference as a journalist, but later found myself billed as a delegate. (Thanks to a misprint, the title 'the Honourable' was bestowed on my name, like the younger son of an earl.) I usually dug out a news story or two in London for my paper, but no scoops. My aim was to learn a bit, meet friends and enjoy myself and, of course, play a few rounds of poker on the side.

I also found myself on several occasions delivering papers to conference sessions from people who were absent. One was Rev. Gordon Moody, an old friend, whose compassionate and sensible support for gamblers in his role as chairman of the Churches' Council on Gambling had done so much to raise awareness of gamblers' problems in Britain before the Gaming Act of 1968. Another was David Kranes, a lecturer in English studies at the University of Salt Lake City, Utah, and a novelist.

I had a curious relationship with Mr. Kranes. I was, in fact, a big fan of his writing. I had once published a piece on creative writing about Las Vegas which extolled Kranes' novel *Keno Runner* as the truest, most imaginative piece of fiction ever written about Las Vegas. It is still (to my mind) the best book there is on life and gambling in Vegas, though virtually unrecognised in America.

I was slightly worried about having to present this paean of praise in front of the author – as a fan one should always keep a respectful distance. I need not have worried, because Kranes failed to show up at the Vegas conference. Instead, I found myself presenting on his behalf the paper he was supposed to deliver to the meeting on 'Casinos as Play Grounds'.

Kranes posed the interesting question: What are the best

ways to 'construct' a 'place' when the activity central to that space is *play?* "There are spaces which, upon our entry, make us feel empowered and expansive emotionally. There are other spaces which can make us feel disempowered and contracted. In other words: certain spaces flood us with energy and make us feel that we are winners; other spaces bleed energy and make us feel that we are losers. Some spaces, when we enter them, feel to be *play . . . grounds* – literally where the urge to play feels spontaneous. There are spaces which, when we enter them, discourage play – where the elements deaden play impulses in the human emotions."

He could walk into any hotel casino, Kranes said, and almost immediately know its survival potential. When Atlantic City was first billed as a destination gaming site, he felt the place was as inherently doomed as Las Vegas was inherently inspired. The essential problem, as he saw it, was the conflict between a casino management's need for space utilisation and the casino patron's need to experience space.

Casino players need to feel 'at home' and also 'enticed' at the same time. He particularly stressed the thresholds of casinos. "Crossing into any power-filled space will feel magical, vital, mysterious. The pulse quickens. The lungs fill. One feels a particular charge in the crossing over . . ."

He then gave his verdict on some of the leading casinos on the Las Vegas strip, circa 1993. Harrah's – middling to poor; The Imperial Palace – fairly good; the Flamingo – good and bad mixed; Caesars Palace – very good. The Mirage – a masterpiece, a textbook on how to design a huge and vaulted airplane hangar-style space and make it feel small, personal, lush, thriving and intimate.

Most players, I think, would agree with these judgements by Kranes and his paper was well received. It may be noted that Harrah's and the Flamingo have subsequently undergone major casino refurbishments.

I looked forward to meeting this insightful author at the next conference, which was in Montreal. And then, dammit, the same thing happened! Kranes failed to show and I was deputed to read his new paper, this time on the aesthetics of casino design. Both his papers were very good, so much so that after the first one, he was hired, I believe, by a leading casino company to advise on design but as yet, I have never met or spoken to the author himself.

Bill Eadington had asked me to give a lunchtime talk at the Vegas conference. These were twenty minute stand-up turns by some widely known personality, like a casino owner, designed to entertain the delegates over their coffee. I dreaded having to undertake this task, but I could hardly refuse Bill, who had done me so many favours, in guiding my journalistic and other writing. Because my party piece says something about the way *personality* affects the running of casinos, I venture to give a summary here, as a counterpoint to the analysis of gambling I gave at the start of this chapter. I began with an analogy with poker.

Poker is a test of character. Everyone knows the odds, but it is the strong characters who win out. And today I want to talk about three characters who have built modern Las Vegas and shaped the modern gambling industry.

The visionary – Steve Wynn. The professional – Jack Binion. And the big-talker – who has not yet got a stake in Las Vegas, Donald Trump, whose patch is Atlantic City.

Okay, I am going to draw a contrast between the personalities whose influence has shaped the modern gaming industry. I'm going to run through this at high speed and leave you to fill in the gaps of the story from your own knowledge of events. As we all know, character is a fundamental aspect of winning and losing. Everyone knows about Steve Wynn. I take it to start with, as a given fact, that Steve Wynn is the most creative personality in modern gaming. What is creativity in casino management? An ability to see new ideas, and develop them and prove they work so that the ideas become part of accepted practice by everyone else and the others pay the innovator the compliment of following him.

Wynn had an insight, an insight if you like into human behaviour. It was this: If you create attractive surroundings, elegant design and well thought out amenities, the customer, the player, will respond. He or she will aspire to fit the surroundings and be worthy of the setting, and be flattered by it all.

If, on the contrary, you fall back on cheap surroundings, pay no attention to the decor, go for the lowest common denominator of comfort, the customer will react accordingly. The result will be negative feelings, regardless of win and loss. Of course it will be mainly loss, we know that, in the nature of casino gambling. But a customer can still lose and be gratified by the experience, and want to come again. Wynn saw all this.

He did it first at the Golden Nugget out in Atlantic City in the early '80s. It set the pattern in flash and filigree and upmarket style. People who played there felt good about it, and the Golden Nugget from a commercial point of view was great. It out-performed every other casino in Atlantic

City while Steve Wynn ran it. The only question was who would come second.

When Wynn sold the property to Bally (who paid much too much for it because they were scared of Donald Trump buying up their shares) he used the money to build his dream casino in Las Vegas, the Mirage. It's old hat to have entertainment, sideshows, or a theme. Now everyone does it. But Wynn set a new standard of showmanship, when he opened the Mirage in November 1989. It defined the modern style, and was copied by other operators up and down the Strip. (Wynn outdid himself all over again in October 1998 with Bellagio.)

It's not the only way to succeed. I turn now to the Horseshoe downtown. I like the Horseshoe a lot. First of all Jack Binion always comps my room in the world poker series, for which I am extremely grateful. Jack Binion is a professional and I think that at his end of the market, Jack is a much underrated man in Las Vegas. He inherited a difficult role to play, to step out of the shadow of his dad, Benny Binion, who started the Horseshoe way back.

Jack Binion's management style is the exact opposite of Steve Wynn. No cabaret, no music, no frills. The Horseshoe is an old-fashioned gambling hall. You put your money down and you go for it. As Benny used to say, "If there's a high limit and the dice get hot, a man can win a lot of money." If you want to bet a million bucks on a single roll of the dice or one spin of the wheel, Jack's your man. Here's how you do it, if anyone here wants to try. You go in with two suitcases. One contains a million bucks in cash, the other is empty. You lay the million out on the dice table. If your bet comes up, you take the million you win and stick it in the second suitcase. If you lose, just leave the cases behind and walk out.

The Horseshoe is not really a high roller's casino, it's an old-style gambling saloon, offering the best value in town – two bucks for a 10-ounce steak dinner. Can't be beat. My point today is that Jack Binion and Steve Wynn mark a kind of bracket of casino operators in Las Vegas.[2]

I come now to my third personality, Donald Trump. I couldn't believe it when I went down to Atlantic City soon after the opening of the Taj Mahal, in the spring of 1990. The place was billed as the eighth wonder of the world. But what did I find? A gigantic structure filled with slot machines, without a trace of human warmth or feeling or humour. Now, I am not one of those who criticise the Donald for being vain, ignorant, loud-mouthed and untalented. Not at all. Anyone who can win Marla Maples must have quite a lot going for him. Though not necessarily in the field of casino management.

We know from Trump's autobiography *The Art of the Deal* how he was attracted to casinos in the first place. He heard on his car radio that two gaming properties here in Nevada, the Hilton and the Flamingo, made as much money as about 40 per cent of the entire Hilton chain. What a revelation. Trump set about acquiring a property himself. He did not know anything about casinos when he got into the business but he looked around, as a property developer would, to acquire a property himself, looking first of all in Atlantic City. Typically, he left it a

[2] Jack Binion sold the property to his sister Becky Behnen, in 1998, so ending a long family feud.

bit late instead of moving into the market right away, but eventually he acquired the building which became Trump Plaza and another that became Trump Castle.

What struck me, as I looked at the contrast between the Mirage and the Taj Mahal, was the duel going on between Wynn and Trump. It was unmistakable in the way the Donald was promoting his operation in Atlantic City – "more than a mirage" he claimed. Here we come to a very personal aspect of the casino industry. Trump came to see himself as the direct rival of Steve Wynn. As they say in bull fighting, *mano a mano*, hand to hand. It may not have been on his part a conscious rivalry but he evidently saw Wynn as the market leader, the front-runner in the industry, and he wanted to emulate him, to out-do him. This explains, so I believe, why Trump was always trying to find a niche in Nevada, to buy his way in here – he acquired stock in the old Golden Nugget when Wynn first ran it, he offered more than once to go partners with Wynn, for example in developing the Mirage. But no deal.

I can illustrate Trump's attitude by telling you a little anecdote about their relationship, which is quite revealing in itself and explains a lot. There was a heavyweight boxing match which Wynn was promoting here. Trump rang Wynn not once, not twice, but a dozen times to make sure he and Ivana were seated as befitted their station in the gaming industry – front row, ringside. These things count, this is how you measure status in this town. And Wynn, who didn't need any of this, who never saw the Donald as a rival anyway, set him in front of himself and Elaine. A magnanimous gesture.

The whole sad story of the Taj Mahal in Atlantic City, in my judgement, is explained by Trump wanting to do out East what Wynn was doing out West with the Mirage. To go one better. And of course because the Donald didn't understand casinos, like Wynn and Jack Binion understand casinos, a whole lot of things went wrong with the Taj, right from the start. As Wynn warned Trump, it was in fact the worst deal of his life. No wonder the Taj rapidly went into chapter 11 bankruptcy.

Okay, maybe the place could rack up a million a day. But if the 'nut', which is what the Donald needed to make on a daily basis to cover expenses, was $1.1m or $1.2m., the outlook was not too bright. As Charles Dickens said in another context: income £20 a year, expenditure £19, 19 shillings and sixpence, happiness. Income £20 a year, expenditure £20 and sixpence, misery. Maybe it will all come right. I certainly hope so.

On the subject of personalities influencing casinos, I want to mention a fourth personality here – a man who never owned or managed a casino, who as an outsider had no direct influence in the gaming industry at all. Gordon Moody is probably well known to many of you here today. As a Methodist clergyman in England he was the first person to stand up for gamblers' interests. He did not take a position either for or against gambling. He simply tried to get to know gamblers and extend a helping hand to people in trouble.

Gordon Moody had a major influence in the framing of gaming legislation in England. He also founded Gamblers Anonymous there. But his lasting legacy is Gordon House, a modest little hostel in south London set up to get problem gamblers off the street and give them a home, to bring them – in Gordon's phrase – back to life. I mention Moody's name in the same breath as great figures in the American gaming industry like Wynn and Binion and Trump to make the point that you don't necessarily have to be a big player with big bucks to make an impact in gambling.

As a young man, as a Methodist clergyman, he had gambling thrust upon him when he was asked to take over the Churches' Council on Gambling. This was an unofficial body in Britain which tried to look at gambling and assess its impact on society and make recommendations about it. Unlike most operators, regulators, moralists and others, Gordon reacted in a direct, simple and human way to the experiences he encountered. This was a generation and a half ago when we didn't understand as much about gambling as we do today. Gordon neither condemned nor encouraged gambling. He just tried, as an open-minded young man at the start of his career, to understand what it was all about.

So he went to greyhound tracks, he went to the Derby – he talked to the ordinary people he met and he saw that gambling had a tremendously positive side to it. This was Gordon Moody's insight. Gambling, so he discovered, wasn't a substitute for sex, a relief from bordeom, a lust for other people's money or a commercial hoax practised on naive people. Gambling was fun and that's why people did it.

But Gordon also saw that gambling had its downside when people went too far and got out of control. His point of view was always to look after the interests of the *gambler*. Simple – but still overlooked all over the world today. The gambler is the guy we should be looking out for. He or she makes it all happen.

In Britain the Government's attitude towards gambling has always been hypocritical. A bit like the Victorians' attitude to sex. We know it goes on, but don't mention it in front of the servants. So far as gambling is concerned, the unofficial British view is: We know it happens, it's an unfortunate lapse of human nature, so we will license it but you mustn't enjoy it too much while you do it. So no entertainment in casinos, no cabaret, no slots apart from a couple of machines per casino (now ten), no music, no drinks at the table and of course the absurd rule whereby you must sign on and declare your intention to gamble 48 hours in advance (now reduced to 24) in case – perish the thought – someone, an American visitor to London like one of you here – might walk in off the street and gamble on impulse.

The British policy, actually, in appointing the Chairman of the Gaming Board, is to look around for someone regardless of whether he or she has had any experience of gaming or has ever even been to a casino – you think I'm exaggerating but it's the literal truth – and stick him or her in charge, with powers of a star chamber, a private court not answerable to public scrutiny or question, which would be the envy of Henry VI in the year 1400 and something. It's the British way. It's called the cult of the amateur. What it really betokens is a superior attitude, 'Nanny knows best', the civil servants in Whitehall know best.

I want to conclude by saying that Gordon Moody discovered an important truth. That gambling controls should not just be for the benefit of the industry, as they tend to be here in Nevada, nor geared to tax revenue, as they are in Atlantic City and elsewhere, nor tailored to some abstract idea of public welfare as in Britain. Gaming controls should be for the benefit of the gambler. In that spirit I conclude by saluting Gordon Moody today and commending his reflections on gambling.

So ended my talk. I was rewarded, after it was over, by the grudging comment of a British casino owner – "Hunh! Better than I thought you'd be."

Society's responsibility towards gamblers who go over the edge and become 'problem' gamblers, which is one of the themes which Gordon Moody raised, has become a live issue today. The gambling industry has finally come to realise that if it doesn't do something to help "those punters with a high propensity to over-indulge", as Eadington put it, it may suffer from governmental interference.

The fate of the tobacco companies is an awful warning. These huge enterprises, having failed to address the downside, the risks associated with smoking – despite the fact that millions of people like to smoke – have been hemmed in and driven back and restricted to the point, almost, of losing the best part of their business. Couldn't the same thing happen to the gambling industry?

Bill Eadington raised the issue at the conference on Gambling and Public Policy held in London in 1990.[3] "For the most part, societies have banned gambling because of the perceived social ills associated with it – the erosion of family responsibilities, the loss of property to undeserving gamblers or gambling operators, misdirection of one's attention from more important endeavors—" Neverthless, very many people still choose to play in one

[3] *Gambling and Public Policy: International Perspectives*, edited by William R.Eadington and Judy A.Cornelius.

form or another. Hence the ambivalent attitude towards gambling.

". . . in many respects, gambling falls into the same category as a wide variety of other commodities, such as alcohol, tobacco, prostitution, pornography, and illicit drugs. All these activities are characterised by three common factors: periodic prohibition or restriction; strong inherent demand; and ambivalent public attitudes resulting in changeable legal status." (As in gambling on the Internet, see chapter 6).

But what is 'play'? The asssumption that gambling is part of the leisure industry – Not a sin! Not a vice! – is one of the themes regularly addressed at the gambling conferences described above.[4] Gaming and entertainment may serve fundamentally different consumer needs and desires, but they have come together at the start of the 21st century. All the major casinos feel they must provide entertainment alongside gambling.

Such entertainment may be integrated into the gaming facility or offered as an added attraction. From the casinos' point of view entertainment in the form of shows, restaurants, rides and spectacles has a double purpose. It brings the public in and, in its own right, can provide as much revenue as gaming itself.

After all, you can't gamble all day and all night. Entertainment provides a break, an alternative. The public wants it and can afford it: in economically developed countries,

[4]Notably by Eugene Christiansen, President, Christiansen/Cummings Associates, Inc. of New York, and Julie Brinkerhoff-Jacobs, Executive Vice President, Lifescapes International, Inc., Newport Beach, California, in their paper of 1994, 'The Relationship of Gaming to Entertainment'.

the consumers demand recreation. Look around – the world of movies, of sport, of videos, is what colours everyday life. Gambling is a part of all that. One might even say that Americans' inalienable right to 'the pursuit of happiness' as expressed in the Declaration of Independence has been given a new spin.

3

Cruisin'

My wife got seasick, so luckily I could play poker all night
Cruise passenger

To sail the ocean blue, playing poker night 'n day, with occasional interludes for snorkelling the coral reef – could anything be more enticing? It was certainly a self-indulgent voyage. To make it seem slightly more serious, I had agreed to give a seminar on 'Tournament Play'. The cruise, for ten days through the eastern Caribbean, was just when the weather in London was cold and miserable.

The trip was organised by June Field, founder of *Card Player* and *Poker Digest*. June Field is a bright, breezy, super-efficient operator, and a strong poker player in her own right. The motto of her company Classic Poker Cruises, promoting poker-fests through the south seas in winter or up to Alaska in the spring, is: 'We pamper our players'. At around $1,300 for the whole trip, with no extras, it offered amazing value.

The Holland-America liner was a big ship, gleaming white, 55,000 tons. It sat like an elongated Hilton Hotel, laid on its side in the water, alongside the dock at Fort Lauderdale, Florida. On board, the poker-playing contingent, some 350 people out of a passenger list of 1,500, headed for their own special room which was hidden away, snugly, under the bows. Ordinary non-poker playing passengers would never even know it existed. Fourteen tables were set out and with a curtain drawn across the picture porthole window, there was absolutely no sensation of being at sea beyond the faint throb of the engines somewhere far below.

Everyone, or nearly everyone, knew each other. There were the hardened poker-cruisers from Vegas; the little old gentlemen, round bald pates like sun-dried berries, from Florida, and their puffy costume-jewelled wives; the narrow-eyed, overweight semi-pros intending to make a turn on the trip; a cheerful gaggle of young women dealers from Vegas and L.A., on a working-vacation, hoping to earn their keep in tokes – at a dollar a hand from the winners; a few odd-balls from places like North Dakota; and me. Already the games were starting up as the good ship *Statendam*, like a gigantic stretch limo, pulled out of harbour and set a steady course down a long, palm tree-fringed estuary to the open sea.

Mildred, a thin, grey-haired old lady in a print dress, came up to me.

"I read all your books, since last year," she told me.

"Gee, Mildred!" (Hope she meant she bought them, not just read them.) I paused to hear some flattering, enlightening comment, such as authors long for.

"And you never got in touch with me!" she protested.

I cast around for a suitable answer. "I'm going to come and see you one day, when I'm in Vegas. How is your life out there?"

Mildred's smile drooped. "My husband's gone." I thought the worst but she rattled on. "Back to Iowa, he got hurt. He was hit by a trolley in a casino."

"Now Mildred, don't you win too much now, will ya?"

All around the card room was the noisy hailing of meeting and greeting, as players scrambled for seats. American friendliness is measured in decibels. The games were limit-raise (as distinct from the British pot-limit) from \$2–\$4 up to \$10–\$20 and \$20–\$40. Small enough for amateurs and enthusiasts, not quite big enough really to hurt. After all, the players had to make their money last over ten days. Classic Cruises company made its profit by cutting each pot. Four bucks a hand, when the pot might be worth four or five hundred dollars, may not seem much. I calculated that over the ten days (there would be no games while the ship was in port) the house would rake from \$60,000 to \$100,000 depending on the action.

My seminar on tournament play had been trailed weeks ahead in the poker cruise brochure. I was depicted as some kind of super-duper poker writer, with a triple-A record. The reality was precisely the opposite: I rarely play tournaments and would not be considered any kind of expert – in London, they would guffaw at the idea. But to an American audience, I was known only by reputation, and therefore regarded, as a foreigner and a writer, like a Russian chess master.

I had, in any case, prepared myself well by reading the available manuals on the subject. Looking around at this collection of genial but more or less hard-bitten players I decided I had better deliver the goods, simply and clearly, and avoid any pretence at being clever or ironic – which would only be taken as bullshit.

For me, the star of the cruise was Poker Jane. Jane was madly enthusiastic about poker, like a poker groupie, talkative and lively, aged around 40-something. Slim, angular, beaky-looking in her horn-rimmed specs, even sexy, despite making no effort to dress up or down, Jane radiated energy for poker like a nuclear reactor. She came from Hicksville, Montana, or somewhere like that, and was on vacation with her husband, who was not a player himself. He ran a radio station and evidently had ample funds to indulge her hobby.

Jane claimed she had won a lot of itty-bitty little tournaments back in her home town. She was thrilled to be in the company of so many serious players, especially someone like me, an author. Unfortunately, one glance at Jane at the table was enough to tell me she could not play the game too well. She was so eager, her enthusiasm got the better of her judgement. How could I tell so quickly? Well, it's like watching someone at tennis. You can see from the first time a player hits the ball, from his or her first forehand drive, if it's drilled full length down the line, or if it's just a lolloping return mid-court. Poker is the same.

'Poker Jane' got her nickname from her e-mail address on the Internet, where she loved to bombard poker experts far and wide with queries about the hands she had played.

"I had ace-jack in the hole, sittin' on the button, 'n I raise, natchally, and the flop comes down king-king-jack. Now how would you play that hyand? I mean I waited for the opener, 'n when he bet, I raised, wouldn't yuh? 'n then on the turn comes another ace, I mean . . ." I love these kinds of stories, I can listen to them for hours, as I did sitting next to Jane on the open deck of the cabin cruiser as we slipped through the aquamarine sea for a day of swimming and snorkelling off Curaçao.

While Poker Jane held forth, her husband Brian sat on the other side, listening. He wasn't into poker and didn't understand what she was up to. He had a high-pitched, squirting laugh, a kind of nervous tic, which punctuated every sentence he spoke. Jane might say, "I was playin' at the cyard room . . . Brian: Hah-hah-hah . . . 'n I wanned to win that sat'llite . . . Hah-hah-ehah-hah . . . 'n then this guy, I din' like him at all . . . Hah-hah-hah-ehah . . ." as if it was the greatest joke in the world.

When we got to the beach, which was a pure strand of white along the tropical shore, Jane showed her high spirits by striding off into the distance to swim naked, Brian trailing behind with towels. I wasn't so smart: I swam into a circle of coral ten feet from shore, and in trying to get through a narrow gap grazed my arms and legs bumping into fire coral. The burns took days to fade.

The other passengers aboard ship were a leathery bunch of retirees. Typical was a conversation (more like a police interrogation really) which I had on my first day in line at the buffet. An old geezer, hearing my British accent, demanded in a whining western drawl, without any preamble: "How hai-i-i' do you play at this poker?" And then without a pause: "Fifty per cent of the British wanna get rid of the Royal Family, issat right?" And as I tried to reply: "What are the Chinese gonna do to Hong Kong?" I tried to answer as simply as possible but I doubt if he understood a word I said. By way of compensation for all these gnarled good ol' boys, I often found myself the youngest old man in the swimming pool.

One especially memorable trip ashore was to Grenada, where we clambered down a narrow mud path through the rain forest to admire a waterfall. It was a steamy, spectacular cascade, hurtling down between the enormous trees and a mass of foliage into an emerald pool, enclosed like a green secret in the primaeval forest. "Don' ya pay no mind to de boa constrictor," said the guide. "When he sees ya, he will jes' gli-i-de away." In awe at the power of nature, we hauled slowly up the path again and got back to the road, breathless, where Poker Jane rushed up to me.

"How did you like—" I started.

"Lissen! I had two queens in the hole in late position. Flop came down 2–2–9. Lou raised me. Last card another queen!"

"Right."

"He cyan't have four deuces, right?"

Brian: "Hah-hah-hah-ehah."

I gestured to the rain forest around us. "Are you going to see the rest of the island?" I inquired of Jane.

"Gotta get back for the tournament, starts at one o'clock!"

What is the essential difference between poker tournaments and cash games?

Poker Jane, in another burst of enthusiasm, had managed to borrow a camcorder from a cruise passenger, to record my lecture, which was staged in a little theatre off the card room.

Ladies and gentlemen, fellow gamblers (I answered my

question), *I have good news and bad news. The good news is: When I have finished talking to you this afternoon,* all of you *will be qualified to win the tournaments that we are holding here on ship. With the expertise you are going to acquire, you can expect to take first place.*

Now comes the bad news. If everyone could share first place, the prize money would be divided equally among all the winners. So all you would get back is your original entrance fee.

I spoke slowly, stressing each point, to get the meaning across. Then I essayed my first joke.

Now I know what you're thinking. You're thinking how can a man who talks the way I talk, with a British accent, possibly know anything about our all-American game? (Laughter)

I'll answer this way. In a recent presidential election in the United States, one of the candidates wondered out loud, 'Why am I here? What am I doing in this campaign?' Good questions, and my answer is that I was sent for by June Field and when the most efficient woman in the world asks you to do something, you just do it, right? I don't apologize for my British accent. As the saying goes, the British and the American people are close friends and allies, divided *by a common language.* (More laughter, it was going to be okay.)

I did not delve into the history of tournament play (which I cover briefly at the end of this chapter), interesting as it is, because it has added a whole new dimension to casino gambling, as well as to poker. Instead, I explained that there were three motives for playing in a poker tournament.

First, you want to win it; second, if you can't win it, you want to take second place; and third – I hope I don't look too pained when I say this, because it's happened to me recently when I played in the World Championship at Binion's in Las

Vegas – third, you do not want to feel you have disgraced yourself in the way that you are beaten.

Now, what is the essential difference between cash games and tournament poker? In a cash game, you are playing for the money on the table and you can please yourself whether to go on, or get up, any time you want. In a tournament, by contrast, you are not playing for the cash on the table. You are playing for a percentage share of all the total entry fees in the event. And you do not win the big prize until you have busted out all the other players in the tournament, every single one of them.

In fact you could be winning virtually all the chips in the tournament, theoretically, and be say, a hundred thousand bucks ahead, against a bunch of players who only have a few hundred, and still not get paid. So, yes, tournaments are different.

The reasons for playing in a poker tournament, I went on, were first, tournaments are fun and second, you can make some money.

I mean fun is fun, but if you can take a few bucks off your friends and travelling companions, isn't that much more fun? Some people don't play in home poker games, because they don't care to win money off their friends. My own formula is different, it is that it's a whole lot better than losing *money to your friends. In tournaments you can win a large prize for a small stake, say $1,000 for 25 bucks.*

Third reason for playing tournaments. It is a sociable activity, where you meet different people in a different way from regular poker games. In a tournament you may be in there, sitting between a world champion on one side and a recreational player on the other side. You are competing against both. The professionals do not automatically win, because the luck of the game can play a big part in the result, rather like the roll of the dice at backgammon.

If the motive for entering a tournament is simply fun, okay. If rebuys are allowed – which means taking a fresh shot at it when you have lost all your chips – go for it. It is usually worth buying in on economic grounds.

If your motive is to preserve your chips and last as long as possible in the event, this is also a perfectably respectable way of playing. You don't take any risks and you sit tight. A player can get a long way like that and feel that he is getting good value for his entrance fee, say an hour or two hours play or more. You are very unlikely to win the event, although this method works well enough, because some risks have to be taken to accumulate chips. No pain, no gain.

The third method is to play fast and loose, taking more or less the opposite tactic of hanging in there as long as possible. Such players want a quick decision, either to hit hard and win a lot of chips, so as to get into a dominant position; or, if that fails, to accept the risk of being busted quickly. You do not lament your fate: you figure either you are going to make a real play for the prize money or the hell with it – if you cannot make it this time, you would actually prefer to be busted early and sit down in a new game. There are always cash games going on around the edges of the tournament tables.

And there is, you will not be surprised to hear, also a fourth way, what we may call the strategy of 'maximum expectation', which is not based on either lasting a long time or making a quick hit. It is based on trying to get into the money. I shall now describe this approach for you in more detail.

We sat on the hot sand in a messy little bay at St. Thomas, one of the US Virgin Islands, surrounded by tourists. The idea was to snorkel the reef, but the organisers had got it badly wrong. There was a tiny space of sea, about the size of a tennis court hemmed in by guide ropes. It was jammed with groups of swimmers, like a school for snorkellers, kitted out in bright orange life jackets. All you could see under water were pairs of legs, row upon row in front of your mask, flapping away like frogs. At the surface, team leaders were shouting out instructions. Beyond the lines, the sea stretched away to the blue horizon, out of bounds. This particular excursion was a rip-off.

Poker Jane was in a mood to unburden herself. Brian was in the water.

"The trouble is he doesn't understyand poker," Jane lamented.

"Who does?"

"I meayun, last night, he comes up to the table, sittin' there watchin' me and he asks: 'Are you winnin'? 'n I say, 'Yes, a little bit,' 'n he says 'Whyn't you stop?' I meayun, what kinda question is that?"

"Can't you explain that a poker game isn't just one hand or one win, it goes on over a long, long time?"

"He cyan't get that. 'n I have been losing on this trip. I set myself a limit of two hun'red a day, 'n I got beyond that. So when I'm winnin' Brian wants me to quit the game. I cyan't do that."

"He's financing you."

"Yeah, he watches me all the time and says 'Why din't you fold that hyand? You knew you were beaten.' I say, 'I din't know I was losin', he coulda been bluffin'. I meayun, you can't play poker that way, can you?"

"No you can't."

"Brian gives me the money to play with. Lucky I gotta rich husban' I guess!"

"You bet!"

"But now I don' know what to do. He doesn't want me to play tonight."

Brian was standing in the water, ten metres off, a big fleshy guy with an amiable, open face. He had pushed his mask up onto his forehead and was leaning down, talking earnestly with a fellow snorkeller.

A large black lady working the beach came by offering thimble-size samples of daiquiri. The sky was clouding over, threatening to rain us off.

I felt sorry for Jane, it seemed such a tiny misunderstanding. "Has Brian got any hobbies, like you play poker?" I asked.

"He's wild about huntin'. He jes' spent $1,500 on a new gun. He'll fly up to Canada to go shootin', once, maybe twice a year. He lerves huntin'."

"He must spend a lot of money on those trips?"

"He c'n afford it. He's very smart, financially. Just as well, hunh, married to me."

"Here's a way you could handle it, Jane," I suggested. "Catch him in the right mood—"

"Hunh."

"No listen, here's an idea for you, how to play it. Suppose Brian gives you, I don't know, say an allowance of $500 a month for your poker, that's $6,000 a year. You open a separate bank account, just for you, to play poker. You can play any time you want, all you want. No questions asked, no problems. If you lose it all in the first couple of months, okay, too bad, you don't play any more that year. If you win, at the end of the year, you n'

Brian can celebrate with a champagne dinner together. He wouldn't have to worry any more about whether you win or lose on a single game."

"Hunh."

"I mean poker is all one game, isn't it, the whole year, your whole life?"

"Ye-e-a-h."

"Six thousand a year isn't such a lot. Probably less than Brian spends on his hunting trips to Canada. Put it that way."

"I don't know. I jes' wanna play tonight is all."

Brian came out of the water and strode up the beach.

"This is a terrible spot," Jane said, "let's get the bus."

It was coming on to rain.

"What were you discussing so earnestly?" I asked Brian who had been standing all the while in the sea, talking away, as we handed in our masks, flippers and life jackets.

"Oh, the whole works! TV, the movies, the economic situation." This time he didn't give his spluttering little laugh between every other word. He sounded serious and thoughtful, a completely regular guy. "The basic question is, can the boom continue?"

I ventured some remark about President Clinton but Brian was off to get a coke for Jane.

On the bus, Brian and Jane and I sat together on the back seat. A burst of tropical rain hit the windows like gunshot. It reminded Jane of her childhood.

"You know, my Mom she's a Baptist, one of those real strict folks, doesn't drink, doesn't smoke, she's against everythin', 'specially gamblin'. You know what Mom said to me? She said, 'When Jesus comes back, he's a-gonna find you sittin' at that ol' poker table, Jane. What you gonna say to Jesus then?'

"I said, 'Mom, when Jesus comes, I JES' HOPE I'M HOLDIN' THE NUTS!'"

Brian looked at her admiringly; he was obviously still in love with her.

"'n you know," Jane went on, "we got married in Reno, n' my Mom came up there. I gave her a roll of quarters to play the slots. I said, 'Go on, Mom, try it.' She put one in the machine and sat there lookin' at it, like the devil was gonna jump out at her. She din' know what was gonna happen. A few minutes later I came by n' she was playing five coins max, and slammin' the handle down, whammo! like a real pro."

Jane sighed. "If I could get back to evens on this trip, I'd give up poker for ever. I did that once. I made a promise to Jesus. 'If I can get even, I'll give it all up.' n' I made it, I really did. But I din' give up poker, after all."

"Hah-hah-hah, ehah-ha."

Think about this. I have outlined the essential difference between tournaments and cash games. The essential difference concerns the value *of the chips you play with.*

In a cash game you sit down with whatever stake you feel comfortable with, let's say $100. If you win, fine. You take the money, play it up or cash it in, play all night long or go home. More to the point, if you lose your hundred bucks, you can pull up another hundred and go on playing in the game for as long as you feel like it.

In a tournament, this is not so. You can win a lot of pots and still not have any financial reward for it.

If a hundred people decide to enter a poker tournament, and *each puts up $100, the total prize money is $10,000. Let's say, to keep it simple, that the winner gets half, which in this case would be $5,000. Second place gets, say, a quarter, which is $2,500 of the total prize fund. Third place gets 10%, and the remainder is perhaps divided between fourth and fifth or sixth places. The exact division doesn't matter so much. What matters is that your $100 in chips is potentially worth $5,000 first prize.*

RISK AND REWARD
PRIZE/CHIPS VALUE
$5,000 /100 = $50 per chip
/500 = $10
/20 = $250
MORAL: NEVER GIVE UP!

WITH REBUYS
$8,000 / 100 = $80 per chip
MORAL: GO FOR IT!

So each tournament chip you have, assuming you start with 100 chips, is worth potentially 50 real dollars at the end. That is your 100 starting stake divided into 5,000 real dollars.

Here comes the paradox. If you win a couple of pots and have not just 100 chips in front of you, but say, 500, you still figure to win the same first prize of $5,000 in the end. So each of your 500 chips is no longer worth $50, as at the start, but only $10. 500 divided into 5,000 = 10.

Your individual chips are actually worth less.

On the other side, suppose you lose two or three hands, and your starting stake of 5,000 is reduced to a miserable 20 chips. Don't despair! Those 20 chips can still, potentially, be turned into *the $5,000 first prize. So the value of your pathetic little stack of 20 has now gone up. Each one of them is worth notionally $250, that is 5,000 divided by 20. Well, I said it was a paradox, and so it is. The more you win, the less each of your chips is worth, and the more you lose, the more – potentially – each of your chips is now worth.*

In fact one single chip can be worth a million dollars.

I retold the famous story of Jack Straus, who had won the 1982 world championship in Las Vegas from a single chip.

When you have a large total of chips, you can take more chances and gamble more easily, because they are not worth so much to you, compared with a player who has very few chips. His bets are going to cost him relatively much more.

So the moral of this story and the whole lesson of tournament play, is: Never give up.

The other important difference from cash games is that in tournament play, when you have lost all your chips, you are out. One chip may be worth a million, but no chips is curtains. It is worth rebuying at least once, because if other players are also rebuying, the total prize will probably go up from $10,000, to say, $16,000. That means a first prize of $8,000. So a player's newly purchased $100 worth of chips now offer an immediate theoretical increase in their value. Each one is now worth not the 50 a player started with, but 80 (as shown in the table).

Naturally you can't extend this principle to infinity. There are other factors to consider: notably how you feel, how you assess your chances, what you can afford, what your spouse or partner is going to say at dinner when you tell him or her how much you have lost, and so on. In a cash game, if you are losing and pull up another 100 you might get lucky and get back to even. In a tournament there is no guarantee that the expense of your rebuys, whatever the chips may be worth in theory, will in fact be justified.

I had a co-lecturer, Lou Krieger, who was talking about Hold 'em to promote his new book. Krieger keeps a low profile at the table but very much wants to win. I spotted him sitting in a little old ladies' game of $2 raises.

"You are relentless!" I mocked him.

Just like on the coral reef, the shoal of colourful fish at the poker tables attracts one or two heavy-eyed predators, looking for a snack. Sure enough, Krieger was dealt a pair of 3s, hit trips on the flop and waited for the turn to re-raise. He took down a pot of $32, with hardly a change in his voice or his expression. As a low-level pro, he paid the same attention to winning in a baby game as in his usual $20–$40 limit game in the poker palaces of Los Angeles.

Later that night he got his comeuppance. A woman leaped to her feet and let out a whoop of triumph. "I hit a straight flush! Whoo-oo-ooh! Against Lou Krieger!" she yelled, broadcasting the happy news to the entire room. Krieger sat there, looking blank.

"Smile!" I told him.

Such are the penalties of authorship at poker. Poker Jane was much impressed by Krieger's reputation, even jumping up between hands to give him a running commentary on her cards.

I gave his new book *Hold'em Excellence* a semi-favourable review. He has made a speciality of low limit Hold 'em. Catching the right cards, in Krieger's analysis, is the least of it. 'Right Game, Right Table, Right Seat' is his formula.

"The most important decision in poker is game selection. As long as you can play it well, choose the game with the weakest opponents . . . Once you're in the right game at the right table, choose your seat carefully. Players who are tight, timid and easy to bluff belong on your left. Loose, skilful aggressive players, as well as those with lots of chips, belong on your right." This is sound enough, in the sense that a good player will always win much more money from weak players than from other winning players.

However, since you cannot always pick and choose in this way, good technique remains the foundation of Hold 'em. The point, these days, when masses of advice is available via poker manuals (to say nothing of the Internet), is that just about everyone knows the opening values of different starting hands and the significance of position – everyone has studied the experts. So what is left? The ability, hardest of all no doubt, to read yourself.

I am sorry to say I remain deficient in this area. Sometimes it is the temptation to drink too much wine at dinner. Sometimes it is playing too late at night. Other times it is persisting when in a losing frame of mind. *You know!*

The night after our abortive snorkelling trip to St. Thomas, I was glad to see Poker Jane was back in action. Brian had evidently come up with more greenbacks. She sat at the table, frowning, not relaxed.

"Hey Jane, baby, how ya doin'?"

She wrinkled her nose. "Cyan't catch a hyand."

I had been losing myself but then in one of those mysterious bursts which come at poker, I hit three high-low hands in a row and wiped out (no skill involved) all my losses. Will you believe me when I say it wasn't the money, which made no difference either way? It was the intoxicating sense of having proved I was a winner. I went out on deck for a while and watched the phosphorescent wake of the liner streaming behind us in the dark ocean.

When I went back in to the poker room, Jane had a huge stack of chips racked up in front of her.

"Hey! Jane! What happened? You're winning all the money!"

"Yeah, I got aces in the box. Twice."

She grinned. Brian was not in sight.

"Why don't you leave the game now?" I whispered. "Go find Brian and go to bed a winner!"

"Are you crazy? Cyan't quit now!"

Okay, let's leave the maths out of it. I am now going to set out a few principles *of tournament play, to back up the strategy of maximum expectation, or giving yourself the best chance of getting in the money.*

I am going to set this out for you in stages, but don't worry. There is no need to listen to all this if you want to take a nap, because I am going to summarize all this wisdom in just one word.

Rather like if someone said, "How do you get to the top of Mount Everest?" the answer would be "Climb!"

So here is my one word for success in tournaments: Aggression!

Agg-ress-ion.

Actually, there is good reason for describing a winning technique in tournaments in different stages, and taking the comparison of Mount Everest.

Because the feature of tournament play is that you start slowly, with very small blinds and antes, which are like the foothills, and then gradually go up higher and higher from base camp, with blinds and antes increasing, until finally you approach the summit, which is the most dangerous part of the climb, because at that dizzying altitude, you have to take the greatest risks, in this case, bet the lot.

The stages of a tournament usually last half an hour or 40 minutes, depending on the speed of the event, when the blinds and antes are raised to the next stage.

Now this first stage, in my experience, is one of the most difficult. The key to it is survival, but not just survival. You have to conserve the chips you started with, certainly, but you also have to make a few chips' profit, to have a chance of getting through the second stage when the blinds go up and the antes kick in.

Let us focus on Hold 'em, either pot limit or no limit. Obviously everyone is looking for pocket aces or kings at Hold 'em. But how often do you catch those sort of hands? Not very often, so you have to play many other kinds of hands.

This first stage is very conservative. People do not want to get busted out in the first hand or the first five minutes, though it can happen. If your aces are beaten, you are cruelly outdrawn, too bad! Just give it your best shot and don't look back.

The most important objective in this first stage is that you can begin to get a read on your opponents, and how they play. It's like the first round of a boxing match when the fighters dance and weave around, sizing each other up.

The moral of stage one, therefore, is survival.

Survival is the point of stage two as well. By now, a few players will be busted out, you hope, and a few others will have bought in. Some players will have quite an intimidating pile of chips in front of them. Give them respect for being strong players, or lucky players. There is no need to take them on.

Instead, try and challenge players with a lower stack of chips than yours. If you can get them all-in, and your attempt to take the pot goes wrong, you are still in there fighting. This is a basic principle of tournament play, which must be understood. Because if it's the other way round, that is, if you are all-in yourself against a player with a bigger stack, and he beats you, you are the one who goes out.

My lecture was interrupted at this point by a message from the Captain via the loudspeaker, reporting our position. A long shoreline, fringed by palm trees, glittered in the heat haze like an advertisement for rum. Paradise Island, originally known as Hog Island, across the bridge from Nassau in the Bahamas, is one of those places I had always longed to visit. It was for years an off-shore haunt of gambling boss Meyer Lansky, and the reputation of its casino was heroically unsavoury.

A little motor launch with a white sun canopy over the seats sped all of us would-be gamblers from the liner, now in dock, across to Paradise Island. The merry Bahamian guide pointed out landmarks such as a castellated white palazzo, with lawns sloping down to the sea, belonging, so he said, to Mick Jagger. The ride took about ten minutes, passing close to the high-arching road bridge, which links the island to Nassau itself.

The man who gave Hog Island its new name was multi-millionaire Huntington Hartford. When he bought the island he intended to turn it into a rich man's playground. Unfortunately for him, he had no talent for business whatsoever and was soon losing money. So he hit on the idea of opening a casino. After failing to secure government approval, he took on a partner with the unlikely name of the Mary Carter Paint Company.

This outfit was generally assumed to be a front for the

money laundering of Meyer Lansky and friends. In another change of name, Mary Carter turned into Resorts International, which lost no time in opening a casino on the island. Hartford was soon ousted, losing most of his $30m. investment.

Now it had a new owner, Sol Kerzner, the operator who created Sun City in South Africa. He set about turning the 800 acre island with its golden beaches and blue lagoons into a full-scale Vegas-style casino resort. Already the Atlantis, ringed by surf and sand, boasted 800 slots and 70 games tables, which put it far ahead of the fly-blown little gambling joints dotted around the Caribbean to tempt cruise passengers ashore.

Cool, cavernous, palely lit, with sharp-eyed pit bosses hunched over mobile phones watching the play, the Atlantis shows the way – high gloss, high tech, high rise – casino resorts are going. The Las Vegas model is staking out the next century.

Meanwhile Poker Jane was still loyally hunched over the camcorder, though whether she could take in a word of my sage advice was another question.

In the middle stages, the rebuys are over. Now we begin to play poker.

Probably about half the original starters are out of it. So in a tournament of a hundred players, you face, say, fifty opponents, with a prize fund, including the rebuys, worth about $8,000 to the winner.

There may be a break here, or a change of tables to fill up empty space. You should use this opportunity to take stock of the chip position in general. Let's say everyone started with 500 tournament chips, for their $100 entry fee. That means there are

50,000 chips in play plus 30,000 in buy-ins which equals 80,000 total, with fifty players left.

So the average holding is 1,600 chips.

Who are the tournament leaders? Are you above or below that level? It helps to know. If the blinds started at, say 10 and 15, and the antes at 5, they will have risen at least three times. The blinds are probably about 100 and 200 and the antes 50. That means in a single round you will be putting up 9 × 50 plus 300 in blinds, which is 750.

And you have, shall we say, the average holding of 1,600 chips. How many rounds can you stand before the antes and blinds eat you up? Barely two rounds.

So sooner or later, you have to take a stand. This shows you why, as I said at the start, a strategy of sitting on your hands and never making a move won't work.

As I said, you must play poker. *You have the advantage of knowing a bit about how your opponents play. And they, in return, know a bit about you. You have the second advantage of seeing how many chips your various opponents have compared with your own position. So you can to some extent pick your shots.*

I can't tell you, no one can tell you, how to play your cards. That is what poker is all about. But here's a good principle to bear in mind: No limit Hold 'em is an all-in game. You must always be prepared to go all-in if you make a move. Ideally, you would like to set your opponent all-in, and make him *decide whether to call. It is far better to be the aggressor than the agressee. As we say in England, 'Get your retaliation in first'.*

If you have very few chips, well under average, you are going to have to take a chance. You have to calculate how many hands you can afford to wait it out before you take a shot at the pot, whether you hold good cards or not.

By now, in any case, the players are dropping like flies and we just hope you are not among them. Because if you have survived, you are down to the last two tables. Like Moses seeing the promised land, you can see the final table looming up. There may be some hardened pros around. There may be some lucky amateurs.

The point is that at this stage, 18 or 20 players, the values change again. You cannot just sit back and hope others will knock themselves out. With antes at say, 100 and blinds at 200 and 400, the game is getting expensive. You have got to steal some antes. Aggression is still the key.

And luck of course plays a big part. You can get outdrawn on aces as on any other hand. But you would far prefer to start with aces and be a 9–2 favourite, wouldn't you?

By the way, if you are outdrawn in one of these either/or situations, do please come over and tell me about it afterwards. Tell me all *about your bad beat and unbelievable bad luck. You'll find me up at the swimming pool, waiting for you, by the deep end. Just stand close to the edge, will you?*

To a few players in the know, tournaments have been a surprising and extraordinarily profitable innovation in casino gambling.

"One evening in 1985," recalls Anthony Curtis, who publishes the excellent monthly *Las Vegas Advisor* listing the town's best bargains, "I took a call that I look back on as one of the most important in my life."

Stanford Wong was at the other end of the line and he came straight to the point. "I'm forming a tournament team," he said. "There are four of us and I think five would make a nice, efficient group. Would you like to play with us?" So began an experience that made Curtis a lot of money and even a little fame.

The point about blackjack tournaments (which started around 1980 with a promotion at the Las Vegas Sahara) is that you don't need to be an expert, or even really to know the game. All a player has to do is to wind up with more chips than the other players. In games where the expectation in normal play is in favour of the house – like roulette, craps or baccarat – it's no good being an 'expert', because there ain't no such thing. An edge of 1.4% against you on the front line bets in dice is an edge of 1.4%. It is a law of mathematics. Even if you take ten times odds (an even money bet on top of your original wager) or if you could afford it, a hundred times odds, the edge though reduced is still against you.

Even in blackjack, which is the one casino game where a counter has a positive expectation, the advantage in tournament play is more or less irrelevant. A player is not trying to grind out a 1% profit over the long haul – and in blackjack it is a very long haul of weeks and months. He is trying purely and simply to wind up with more money than his rivals in a *short run* gamble. In the short run minuscule percentages don't help.

So where does the skill come in tournaments? In that much derided concept 'Money Management'.

The guru of tournament play in blackjack is a man called Stanford Wong, in his private life a serious-minded mathematician resident in California. Wong has been the dominant writer on blackjack over the past couple of decades. His book *Tournament Blackjack* (1987) spilled the beans, for anyone who wanted to know how to win tournaments.

In the judgement of Arnold Snyder, known as 'the Bishop' throughout the realm of blackjack in tribute to his ex-cathedra judgements on the game in his newsletters, *Tournament Blackjack* is a classic. He predicted that in the literature of blackjack it would stand alongside the two professorial texts, Ed Thorp's *Beat the Dealer* (1962) and Peter Griffin's *Theory of Blackjack* (1979). It was certainly the first book to explain tournament strategies in detail.

Wong bankrolled a team of tournament players (five men and a woman) in December 1985, to follow his playing and betting strategies. They played not only in blackjack tournaments but craps, Keno and handicapping (horse race) events as well.

"Within one year's time," the Bishop enthused, "the six members of the team had taken no less than eight major tournament prizes totalling well over $200,000. Considering the relatively few hours of table play involved [compared with the 10 or 12 hours a day spent at the tables day after day by conventional blackjack teams] Wong's tournament team must be viewed as one of the most successful legal team gambling ventures in history."

Peter Griffin, who used to teach maths at the State University of California, Sacramento, once applied Eugene McCarthy's comparison of politicians with football coaches to playing blackjack: 'You have to be smart enough to understand the game and dumb enough to think it matters'. He studied the team in action.

"It was fascinating to watch the way they squeezed out the other contestants, who had no idea of what they were up against," he reported. "The other players were like lambs going to the slaughter." (An apt metaphor because in his classic treatise *Beat the Dealer*, Thorp had succeeded in reversing the famous casino dictum, 'When a lamb goes to the slaughter, it *might* kill the butcher. But we always bet on the butcher.')

"For blackjack tournaments, tournament skill is considerably more important than blackjack skill," Wong introduced the subject. "In fact, counting cards is so unimportant in a blackjack tournament that often I don't even bother with it, even at single deck." Which is almost like a poker player saying, 'I don't even look at my cards, I just bet the hand regardless.' What does it really mean?

"Getting an edge in a blackjack tournament for the most part means correct money management – betting the right amounts at the right times," Wong explains. In a blackjack tournament there are a series of 'rounds' in which winning players advance to the finals, rather like a tennis tournament. If there are say, 140 players entering the event there might be 20 tables.

The two or perhaps three players at each table with the most money remaining after a given number of hands, for example, 30 hands, advance to the next round. If there were three qualifiers, these 60 players who came through the opening round of the tournament would then repeat the process at the second stage, which might comprise, say, 10 tables. And so on, up to the final table. The player with most chips left after the last hand has been dealt out is crowned tournament winner.

Here is a simple example. Coming into the final hand of a blackjack table, where one winner advances to the next stage of the tournament, you have $1,000 in chips and your main rival $990. How do you bet?

Answer: if it is up to you to bet first, you bet $990! This will force your opponent to bet his entire stack. If you both win the hand, you will still be in front (and he won't have any more chips to double down or split if he catches the right cards). If you both lose the hand, you will still have your nose in front. If you lose and he wins, you will be beaten. But you have to bet, to force the issue – Win or Bust is the only way to go. If you do not bet, your challenger could place a small bet of say $11 and overtake your stack of $1,000.

By contrast, if it is up to your opponent to bet first, you simply match his bet – even to the extent of betting the maximum he has, $990 – to keep your lead. The count of the cards has absolutely nothing to do with it! The expertise of Wong's team may be judged by a tribute to one of their member's play from an opponent who never forgot it: "About five years ago while playing in a blackjack tournament, I had $1,400 and change going into the last hand. Anthony Curtis was at the same table. He counted me down so perfectly that he beat me by exactly one dollar."

Or take craps, the dice game. Personally I have aways considered craps a fun but ultimately pointless gamble. It is fun because when the dice are 'hot' all the players involved are on a roll. The whole table is as one, rooting for the shooter to hit his point. When the number is thrown, the crush of players pressing around the rail explodes in a roar of delight, which carries way across the casino floor – a burst of glee, unique in gambling, because everyone feels part of it.

I once saw a grateful high roller, who had been betting in thousands, press a hundred dollar chip into the hands of a bemused small-time shooter who had made a long run of winning passes, betting in fives and tens. But craps is pointless, too. You cannot beat the game, except in the short run, and that is all there is to it. Or so I thought.

Wong begins his treatise on tournament craps with the unemotional (but stunning) comment: "Whether I win or lose in my bets against the casino does not matter much; what counts is whether I win more (or lose less) than the people I am competing against."

Imagine! It doesn't matter whether you win your bets – what a revolutionary thought for a craps player or any gambler! It seems to turn the whole point of gambling upside down. You can bet on the Pass line, that the shooter will throw a 7 or hit his point, or you can bet on the Don't Pass line, that the shooter will 7-out – and it makes no difference.

Getting an edge in a casino game tournament depends on correct money management, Wong explains. That is, betting the right amount at the right times. It follows that the most important skill required to win tournament prizes is being able to tell how many chips your opponents have. Wong has a big edge in a craps tournament if he can tell precisely how he stands compared to his rivals. This is not so easy but comes with practised observation. Craps is a complicated game at the best of times. In top-notch tournament play it is far more complex still. Anyone who is not a quick calculator can forget about it.

"Poker tournaments," Wong notes, "are won by poker skill. Tournament skill has little to do with who wins a poker tournament." Well, yes and no. The skills required in winning a poker tournament, as I hope I have shown, are in fact quite different from the skills required in playing a cash game. In poker tournaments there is also an element of what one might call 'Wonging' it, assessment of your opponents' chip standings.

Stanford Wong has had to endure the fate of other authors of 'how to' books on gambling. Their work has shown all the other players out there how to improve their game, and thus made it harder for the original author to exploit his own expertise to win. "Tournaments are now much tougher to win," Wong told me. "The technique hasn't changed over the years, but you have to be more aggressive early on to beat your opponents, not wait until the end game."

And so you reach the peak of Everest, the Final Table! Congratulations! It's been a long haul but there you are, with eight other players. Everyone is happy and relaxed and the tension of the last few minutes has been replaced by a lot of joshing and joking. Great! But your job has only just begun.

Two or three players will have very small stacks of only a few hundred chips. Remember, there are 80,000 chips in play. Some players will have skyscrapers of chips which look very intimidating. Don't worry – you only have to double through one time and you will be up there with the leaders. Conversely, you only have to be beaten all-in one time, and you will be out. All you will get (like a death rattle) is a sympathetic round of applause.

So, rule one. Attack the small stacks. Everyone else will be doing this too, and the small stacks know that they have only one chance to defend themselves. It's ruthless, but that's the game we all know and love.

Two: having reached the final table, some players will be so happy they won't be concentrating quite so hard. They will feel they have made it into the money, and that's good enough.

That's not how the professionals feel! They want to win the tournament. They will be playing very aggressively and using all their skills.

As the small stacks get knocked out, so the field is reduced, to eight, seven, six, five players. Short-handed play is a tough game. You have to be aggressive, sure, but you also have to know your man. The values all change. A bare ace can be a powerhouse. A check raise is terrifying. A small pair looks good, but not against two overcards. By now you must have established your own style of play so the others respect you and, we hope, fear you. So when you bet out, they know you mean business.

Chuck Thompson once wrote a brilliant article, reprinted in Tom McEvoy's Tournament Poker, *entitled 'Where the Fox and the Farmer Meet'. The foxes are on a steal, snapping their teeth at every pot. The farmers are trying to conserve what they have safely. The foxes are playing to win. The farmers are trying to stay in there.*

Whether you are a fox or a farmer is a matter of temperament. The main thing is: you are in the money, you have had a good run and a lot of fun. Isn't that what poker is all about?

When it gets down to the last three players, there is always a temptation to make a deal. If the first prize is say, 50% or $8,000 and the second prize is 25% or $4,000, isn't it better to agree a split, and take $6,000 each? And what about the third place spot, worth say 15% or $2,400? Shouldn't this player be cut in?

There is nothing unethical, in my opinion, about these kinds of arrangement, if they are done honestly and openly between the players. It all depends on the relative chip positions. If the tournament leader has, say, 90% of the chips and the other two only have a few hundred between them, obviously he is not going to make a deal. But if the chips are more or less equally divided between the players, and it is a friendly little tournament like we are holding on board ship, a deal makes sense. The players would each take, say 30% of the prize money for the first three places, and play for the final 10%.

When there are just two finalists left in, it has happened in the World Series that one of them feels so strongly that he (or she) wants the honour and prestige of the title, and the gold bracelet, that he has been prepared to give up part of the prize money, as an inducement to the other player to take second spot. This, I think, is going too far – it devalues the title and is against the spirit of poker.

Finally, here is a case where a top player completely failed to understand the money situation in the final of the World Championship of 1993, by trying too hard to win.

Three players were left in at the final table, Jim Bechtel and John Bonetti, each with about a million dollars in chips, and a third player Glenn Cozen on less than $100,000. The blinds were up to $3,000 and $6,000, so it was obvious that Glenn Cozen was only moments away from being busted out.

Bechtel on the button raised with a pair of 6s. Bonetti, who had A-K in the hole, and Cozen on the big blind both called. The flop came down K-6-4.

Cozen and Bonetti checked, Bechtel bet $85,000 and Bonetti, who is a very aggressive and totally fearless player, check raised $95,000. Cozen of course folded. Bechtel on three 6s just called.

On the turn Bonetti made a huge bet to put himself all in. Bechtel called and his trips stood up.

To his amazement, Cozen – and this is the point of this story – an innocent bystander to this clash, found he had unexpectedly backed into second place in the tournament. He won $420,000 instead of $210,000.

That crazy bet by John Bonetti cost him $210,000 in real

money. He had forgotten, in the heat of battle or the excitement of the moment, that what they were really playing for was the prize money, not the tournament chips as such – the distinction I explained at the start of this talk.

FINAL TABLE DISASTER

FINAL THREE

1. Jim Bechtel	*1,000,000 chips*
2. John Bonetti	*1,000,000 chips*
3. Glenn Cozen	*100,000 chips*

COST per ROUND
$1,000 antes, $3,000 + $6,000 blinds

HANDS

1. Betchel	*(button) raises on 6–6*
2. Bonetti	*(small blind) calls on A–K*
3. Cozen	*(big blind) calls*

FLOP K–6–4
Bonetti and Cozen check. Bechtel bets on trip 6s.
Cozen folds. Bonetti check raises.

TURN
Bonetti goes all-in for the rest of his million.
Bechtel matches it.

ACTUAL DISTRIBUTION of PRIZE MONEY

1. Bechtel	*$1,000,000*
2. Cozen	*$420,000*
3. Bonetti	*$210,000*

Finally I summed up the differences between tournament play and cash games.

It is a strange thing that some very strong tournament players cannot win in cash games, and some very consistent winners in cash games simply cannot cut it in tournaments. Why?

Here are five pointers.

One: The length of a tournament is very important. Most tournaments are one-day affairs. Here on ship, they will last four or five hours I imagine. The faster the blinds and antes go up, the harder it is to make your chips last and wait for good cards. Some people haven't got the sense of timing required, that combination of patience and aggression. The extreme case, of course, is satellites, when it is a real shoot-out, because the whole thing is over in an hour or so.

Two: position. Use of antes in addition to the blinds means there is more money in pots at the start of each hand than there usually is in cash games. The money is there, if you can steal it, which puts a premium on opportunism and courage.

Three: psychology. In money games, a player will often go on tilt when he is losing and – let's admit it – this makes the game much more attractive for the other players at the table. In tournament play, going on tilt usually lasts about one hand unless the player involved is very lucky.

Four: changing your style. As I described, this applies through all the different stages of the event. You have to watch for this, and be able to change gears. In a cash game you can win the money and go home, or you can pull up more money and try to get your losses back. Also, you can pick your opponents in your choice of table. In a tournament you do not have that option. You have to sit where you're told.

Five: At the final stage, relative chip positions are crucial. If you have a lot of chips, you can dominate the table. If the tournament prizes are much higher for the last three places, you can sometimes hang in there on virtually no chips, not playing a hand, just hoping that another low stack will go bust before you do.

I once played a little stratagem like that against my English friend and co-author Tony Holden. We were down to the last two tables in Binion's press tournament, sitting at separate tables. We had bet a bottle of champagne on who could laster longer. We each of us had only enough chips for one more big blind. As the deal came around, I managed to stall and hold up my play for a few moments, while Tony was putting his chips in and in those few moments, he went bust just before I did.

Well, you've got to get it where you can, haven't you?

And on that note I stopped.

I was lounging at a beachside restaurant in Fort Lauderdale, musing about the cruise. The sea was deep, deep blue with a broad streak of paler blue, like a bar of paint across a canvas, running all the way along the strand. A three-mast yacht rode at anchor, way out. Tanned young guys and girls in bright beach clothes served the tables. I had fresh tuna and salad and swigged down several glasses of Chardonnay. Life is not all bad beats!

But then I was struck by a second thought. Have I really learned anything about poker since my first visit out West, at the age of twenty-two, the age of these kids? Well, obviously, yes from a technical point of view. But as for being a *better* player, the truthful answer has to be: Yes, but not much. Fewer mistakes, but not enough 'gamble'. I did not play too well on the cruise as a whole. I was too prone to worry over my mistakes instead of celebrating my wins – an habitual fault. My faults, like Poker Jane's, are probably ineradicable – better make the best of them.

Next time I was in America I rang Jane, to see if she and Brian might fly over and meet me in Vegas, when the World Series was on. She sounded a bit evasive. They had spent a bundle of money on decorating, she explained, and couldn't afford to take the trip.

Then I got an e-mail, giving me the real story. Jane had given up poker!

"I need to tell you I am not gambling these days. I decided to take a year off from it, as I was becoming way too involved. I didn't want it to get to the point where it was controlling my life. I never had a problem with live poker but sometimes I did have a tendency to go overboard with the video poker."

Instead, Jane sent me her story entitled, 'Diamonds Are a Girl's Best Friend', which had been published in *Card Player.* It began, naturally, with a poker game.

"I sat down in seat No.5 and asked the chip runner to bring me a rack of white. He grabbed the bill from my hand as I glanced around the table to assess the competition. Most of the regulars were there: Big Dog, Mailman, Nyles, Rusty, among others . . ."

Sitting next to the dealer she sees a new face, probably a travelling salesman, sitting in on the game to pass the time. She (the protagonist of the story) sits quietly, folding her cards, waiting for a good hand, when the stranger perks up.

"I thought you were here to gamble, little lady."

This annoys her. "I try to take the gamble out of poker, sir," she tells him. The stranger's manner at the table is thoroughly unpleasant, grumbling, throwing his chips about, calling for deck changes, new set-ups and decisions. Shortly, she picks up 6–3 of diamonds in the big blind and as there is no raise, gets to play the hand.

The flop is no help but it does contain two diamonds. She calls the stranger's bet, the others all fold.

"Finally decided to gamble, little lady?" he chortled.

This riles Jane (the little lady in the story remains nameless). "I am as courteous a player as you'll ever want to meet," she confides. "I never abuse a player or a dealer. I tip the chip runners, brushpersons, dealers, cocktail waitresses – everybody. I never try to impose my opinions on my friends at the table . . . I don't lecture, criticize or gripe [if only everyone in casino card rooms was like her!] – and I don't like to sit for hours and listen to others do it, especially this guy."

So she decides to get him. The next card doesn't help, but she comes out betting just the same and when he hits back – "Raise, little lady," he bellowed. "Get out, I got the nuts!" she goes mad and re-raises on her flush draw. "I must be nuts!" she tells herself wryly. The whole table is watching her.

But it's all okay – the diamond comes on the river and Poker Jane socks it to him.

Of course there's a big element of wish-fulfilment in her story, and why not? Poker Jane's essential niceness comes out in her last paragraph. "I felt sorry for him, as he'd lost a bundle, but I suppressed those feelings of pity long enough to say, as he walked away: 'If you are ever in town again, look me up.' Then I stacked my chips."

Jane told me, when I congratulated her on her story, that she intended to play poker again next year. "In fact I am planning to play in the World Series of Poker next year, as I always said I would for my fiftieth birthday . . . If I am not too old!"

In life, as in poker tournaments, it is sometimes a good idea to change gears.

4

Tuesday Night

I started this series, subtitled 'Ups and Downs of the Amateur Game', for a new magazine which unfortunately folded after five issues, without paying its contributors. All the characters depicted in these games are fictional (more or less) including Dave.

For any reader who wants to follow the hands in detail, may I recommend using a pack of cards? The hands are a bit complicated, as they usually are in these sort of home town games, but instructive.

1

Gerry is showing three clubs in a seven card high-low hand.

I don't know which way he's going.

This is a strictly home town school. Gerry is a bigshot company lawyer with more money than you can shake a stick at.

For him, poker is an amusing break from dealing with figures in the million pound bracket all day long at the office.

His second car is a Porsche. The Ferrari is too racy for driving downtown. So the money he wins or loses at poker is not too significant.

On the other hand, baby . . . When the big loser winds up paying out £700 or £800 or in worst cases £1,000 on the night – which is not a big sum, but just enough to hurt – you kind of take it seriously.

I do, anyway.

"Gerry, what are you foolin' at?" I inquire. "Can't you see my low hand out there!"

This sort of verbal banter is par for the course in this game.

Here's how the hands look on seventh street:

Gerry: (x x) A♣ 7♣ 9♣ 5♦ (x)
Dave: (7♥ 3♥) A♥ 5♥ 9♠ 3♦ (8♠)

There's too much money in the pot to fold and I still don't know which way to go. But first comes a 'change' card. We love to have a final change of card in this school when the hand is completed – £5 to change a card face-up, £10 to replace a card in the hole. It pumps up the adrenaline. Or you can stand pat without a change.

Gerry threw a fiver into the pot and pushed his 9♣. Now I *know* he's going for low.

We push in sequence for new cards, so I have the advantage of seeing Gerry's buy. He catches a 4♥.

I was sitting on a terrible hand. An 8-7 low, which did

not figure to improve because most of the low cards had already gone, and a four flush to the high.

But with Gerry pushing the way he did, I figured I was safe enough to win half the pot calling high. So I discarded my 3♦ (duplicated by another 3 in the hole) with a flourish, to give him the impression I was going high.

I caught another heart, the jack, which gave me a somewhat fortuitous flush. I didn't take Gerry's hand too seriously for the high end.

Now comes the final round of betting which we both took to the full, £10, plus a maximum of three raises. I didn't want to kill any of the raises, which you can do by betting just £1, because it would show weakness.

By now everyone else had dropped out, even Rodge who likes to play every hand to the death regardless. He is quite content to lose week after week in return for the camaraderie of the guys. Besides, he sold his business a couple of years ago for £5m. so doesn't care about the money either.

Dave cares. I'm employed in a government agency with loads of prestige and a risible salary. The pot is now worth over £200.

One coin in the hand for low, two for high, and three for both ways.

"Go get him Dave," says Rodge, sitting opposite me. Rodge is a convivial sort of guy, with a woman problem. He has a great way with all the ladies he knows, bar one: his wife.

There is one woman in the game. Rodge always sits next to her, to flirt with her. She's a pretty, fluffy lady in her early 30s who has some sort of customer relations job in a bank downtown.

"Don't be intimidated, Gerry!" she intervenes.

God knows how she got mixed up in this suburban school of would be high-rollers. In fact Flora (known as Flor-baby or Flor-pops in this school) is a pretty good player. In deference to her presence, the guys always apologize after using the F-word.

Thus: "F--- it, I needed that case deuce! Sorry, Flor-baby."

Gerry and I extend our closed fists. Surprisingly, we have both gone high. Surprising to me that is.

"Go get him Dave!"

Now there is a further round of betting *after* the declaration.

Didn't I mention that? In this crazy school we bet again, after the hands are declared high or low, on the eventual result. A mandatory first bet of £20 followed by up to three raises.

Can be a bit bumpy, but you get used to it, as Winnie the Pooh said, on going downstairs.

If two people are declaring and one goes high and the other goes low, that's the end of the betting. If three people are in, and one goes high and the other two go low, the high man gets a free roll!

Well, it works out the same for everyone in the end.

Now Gerry bet £20 at me.

"Do you want to split it?" I ask. This sort of deal is allowed in this school. In fact, anything is allowed, including looking at other people's hands if you are not in the pot yourself.

"No!" says Gerry smirking. "Thanks for the offer."

I can't fold my flush for a lousy £20, obviously. So I try and push it.

"Okay, £20 more, to teach you a lesson." I am hoping he'll say, 'OK, let's split.'

"What's going on?" demands Rodge. "Are you two in bed together?"

"No thanks!" says Gerry.

"What a thought!" giggles Flora.

"I'll take a full raise," announces Gerry calmly, flicking in another £20 note. We play with notes, not chips. Saves writing out cheques.

Now I know my flush to the ace-jack won't stand up. Reluctantly I fold. He must have hit a hidden full house. Gerry scoops the pot.

"What did you have?" I inquire. This is also standard practice in this game.

"Flush!" says Gerry triumphantly.

"Good hand, Gerry," I congratulate him. "What was it, ace-king?"

"Ace-ten," says Gerry flipping his hole cards.

I mess my cards, seething inwardly. How could I be so stupid as to put down an ace-jack flush, goddammit. The next deal is already on. Five card high-low, roll each new card up or down, with two changes at the end.

"I thought you were going low," I explained to Gerry, "when you discarded that nine of clubs."

"I hit a six card flush," he says. "That's why I discarded the nine of clubs, to make you think I was going low, and call high against me."

"You're trickier than a creek of alligators," I congratulate him.

"Yeah, but they have a nicer smile," says Rodge.

2

New player in the game tonight.

Everyone is curious. What's he like? Does he know how to play, for Chrissake?

"Hi Harry! Good to see ya."

"Where ya from, Harry?"

"San Carabinas."

"Where the f---'s San Carabinas?" Rodge inquires. "Sorry, Flor-baby." Rodge makes the routine apology for using bad language.

"Don't worry," says Flora, the only lady in the game, and quite a fast little number, "I never heard of it either."

"It's down south," explains Harry. "New commercial centre."

Dave takes Gerry, the host tonight, to one side, whispers: "Who is this guy?"

"My new bureau chief, down south."

"He okay?"

"'course he's okay. Whaddaya mean? Think I'd hire a shmuck to run my office?"

"Sorry, Gerry, only asking."

"I wouldn't hire you, Dave, if you were the last man in town," Gerry affirms. "Last man on earth. That's for sure."

"Okay, okay, just wanted to know if the new guy understood the game."

"Harry!" Gerry bawls across the room, "Dave wants to know if you understand the game! Lissen, *no one* understands this game," hoots Gerry.

Gerry has the authority that comes from not having to

worry about money. He is a company lawyer, a big hitter, and plays poker to let off steam out of court. We're playing in his den. Pictures of Marilyn Monroe and other movie stars round the walls. Signed photos.

"Except Colin," I interpose. "He understands the game."

"Yeah, 'n I'm not telling," says Colin. He is the mathematical wizard of the school. "Can we get started, or do you want to make polite conversation all night?"

We deal around, first one-eyed jack to start, and it falls on the new player, Harry.

He is a pudgy looking guy with cropped grey hair and rimless glasses.

"Dealer's choice, right?" he inquires.

"That's it."

"Okay, here's a game we play in our school. It's called Route 66."

"Yeah?" everyone draws in their breath. A new game is fun, but a new game on the first deal? Hunh.

"Yeah, goes like this," explains Harry. Everyone gets five cards."

"Right." We can figure that part.

"Then I deal out two rows of five cards, and turn them up one at a time. Any card in your hand that matches a card in the top row, you discard it. You're trying to get as low a total as possible. Face cards count 10, the others you just count the pips. So if you're left with 8-7-6 say, you got a total of 21."

"Jesus!" exclaims Colin, "I thought we were playing poker. You know, that funny old game people used to play?"

"Aw right Colin," says Gerry, "take it easy, we'll get there."

"Yeah, and the second line, that makes a regular poker hand, a high hand," Harry goes on. "You just combine it with the cards in your own hand. So if you've got two kings and there's two kings on board, you got quads."

"What!" shrieks Colin, "You got ten cards to build on?"

"Simple, isn't it?"

Colin blinks. "Simple is the right word."

"One other thing," adds Harry. "You change one card at the end. If you catch one that matches a card in the low line, you discard it. You could wind up with a total of zero!"

"I can't believe this," moans Colin.

"Oh come on," soothes Flora, doing her Florence Nightingale act, "you can work it out, Col!"

"Go ahead and deal!" commands Gerry.

I don't want to play this hand at all, but what the hell. I'm dealt a great low, 2–3–4–6–6. The first upcard is a 4, which I discard, so I'm already down to 17 points.

The betting is tentative, but everyone strings along.

Then comes a 3, which I also discard. Now I've only got 14 points.

"What happens if you don't discard one of your cards when it's matched, by mistake or something?" Rodge asks.

"You forfeit the pot."

"*Shee-it!*" shouts Rodge. "Sorry, Flor-pops." He throws a 3.

An ace of diamonds is showing on the high line of cards, otherwise nothing.

Next up-card on the low side is a 5, only one 5 drops. A second ace appears on the high side.

I'm still very low.

Fourth and fifth cards bring no change.

Low line: 4♣ 3♥ 5♠ Q♠ K♣
High line: A♦ 10♣ A♥ 8♦ J♦

Dave, that's me, Mr. Nice Guy, figures he's good for low. No one has a 3, 4 or 5 in his hand, because of the discards, and two aces are out on the high hand. So to beat Dave's total of 2–6–6 =14, a player would have to hold all the aces and 2s, which seems highly unlikely, or some combination like A–2–2–6 or A–2–2–7. They're all holding four cards still.

I've only got three.

So I raise. Three callers, Colin, Gerry and Harry who started this mess. Realistically, only one of them can be low. I sort of feel it's Harry, because he looks pretty confident. Now, in a delayed reaction, he discards a king which matches the last up-card, so he's down to a three-card hand like me.

He bets, Colin and Gerry raise, Harry merely calls so I take the last raise to try and look like I've got the nut low.

Next there's a change of card. "No thanks," I announce, "can't afford it." I don't figure to improve on my 6s.

Gerry pays £10, throws a card from his hand and takes a new one, Colin stands pat on a hand of five cards, Harry changes a card and catches a 5, which he discards on the low line.

"How many cards've you got now Harry?" I inquire with a dry mouth.

"Oh, just a wee pair," he answers, unblinking behind his rimless glasses.

"Hope it's a high pair."

"Declarations!" We all stick our fists out, one coin for low, two for high, three (unlikely) for both ways.

As expected, Gerry and Colin are high. There's another round of betting now, £20 and three raises of £20, just to rub salt in it. Can I possibly go low against Harry's two-card hand? After all, he knows this game and I don't.

My total of 14 still feels pretty good. I don't believe he's got some fantastic low. The aces are almost certainly in the high hands, so if he hasn't got a 2 down there, I'm probably okay. Anyway it's the first hand of the night, so I call.

"What've you got?" I ask.

"14!" He shows 7–7.

"Nice hand," I tell him. "We split the low half, quartered up. But we don't lose anything with four players in."

Colin turns his cards. "Four aces!" he announces quietly.

"Tough one," says Gerry. "Straight flush here."

"Whaddaya talkin' about!"

Gerry spreads the 7–9–10♦ to go with the 8♦ J♦ on board. "I hit the middle pin 9 on the change card," he explains.

Colin turns very pink and says nothing.

Flora turns to Harry, the new player in the school: "You call this game Route 66?"

"Yup."

"If you'll excuse me saying so, Harry, it's one helluva f-----g road."

"Flor-pops!" Rodge expostulates. "Language, please."

3

"Have you seen the new girl in Gerry's office?"

"What new girl?"

"The one with bazooms like nuclear missiles," says Rodge smirking.

We always apologize to Flora, the only lady in this merry little suburban game, after some sexual innuendo.

There are quite a lot of apologies heard during the night.

We've played every Tuesday on and off since time began, so everyone knows everybody's lifestyle, let alone their playing habits, inside out.

"The lady in question is my new personal secretary," Gerry informs Rodge, who is renowned as a ladies' man anyway, "and if you come within a hundred feet of her, you're dead."

"Listen," demands Cool Colin, "does anyone know what the game is? Is anyone paying attention to the dealer?"

He holds the deck in mid-air.

"Or are we going to spend the evening discussing Rodge's sexual hang-ups?"

"Colin, dear boy," says Rodge, "an evening would not be nearly long enough to do justice to that fascinating topic."

"Deal, dammit!" I tell Colin, "Assert yourself!"

"Five card high-low, roll 'em, with a change at the end, low man must bet," announces Colin. He is a mathematician who knows the odds to three places of decimals, but unfortunately (or fortunately) has never realized that odds don't mean a thing if you ain't got people sense.

I get a good starting hand, A♣ 4♥, and roll the 4 face up leaving the ace in the hole.

It's up to me to bet against a nondescript lot of 8s and 9s and Qs, but I bet the minimum to keep them all in.

Next card gives me a 5♣, another beauty. I roll it face up. Still best showing for low, so I bet it.

Four callers, including Rodge who is a man who likes to take chances. He can afford to, having sold his business a year or two back for £5m.

He's showing Q♥ 5♥. I put him in a queen in the hole, no worry.

My next card is a bad one, a Q♠. I decide to roll it just the same, because of the deception value of keeping my ace down in the hole. I can pair it on fifth street, or keep it down there if I catch another low card.

Fourth street looks like this:

Dave: (A♣) 4♥ 5♣ Q♠
Rodge: (?) Q♥ 5♥ 7♥
Flora: (?) 8♣ 9♠ 8♦
Gerry: (?) 9♥ 7♣ J♦

I bet the limit, which is £5, Rodge calls and Flora raises – quite rightly. She's probably got two pairs, and wants to push the high hands out.

Gerry sees that it is going to cost him a bundle to see this hand through and decides he ought to fold. But he can't resist it, drawing to an inside straight.

"Just one more time!" he announces, throwing his £10

in the pot. We play with cash because it's simpler than writing cheques.

I'm still showing low so I re-raise. The others call. Now there's over £150 in the pot.

My next card is another bad one, a 10! Disastrous in fact. So I roll the ace to show power and hide the 10 in the hole. Still looks like a pretty good hand with a draw to come.

Rodge calls showing a worse low, no flush any more.

Flora has hit a second open pair showing 8s and 9s, so she is obviously going high. She raises.

Gerry folds reluctantly. "Look at that!" he complains to Colin, next to him but out of the pot, flashing his hole card. Probably had a 10 for a straight draw, but figures Flora has most of the 8s.

I take the last raise and Rodge still calls.

This is bad news for me. I just want to split the pot and get out of it with my half.

"What's going on Rodge?" I inquire meekly. "You still fixated on the new girl in Gerry's office?"

"Don't you worry about my love life, sweetie," says Rodge, "I'm not thinking about that. I'm thinking about beating the bejesus out of you on this hand. Sorry Flor-pops!"

As high hand, Flora has to make her change of card first. £5 for an up-card, £10 for a card concealed in the hole.

"I think I can afford to make a generous gesture," says Flora. "Hit me, Colin." She throws £10 in the pot and pushes her hole card.

Now it's my turn. Obviously, I have to push the queen. If I'm going to persuade Rodge to fold, I know I've got to look like a cinch low on the board. So

I throw the queen . . . and catch another lousy stinking queen!

"Oh, tough luck Dave!" says Rodge with mock sympathy. "Did you see that, guys? A queen for a queen! Did you ever?"

I utter a silent curse. For once I'm at a loss for words.

Now Rodge pushes his high card, the queen. And catches an easy 10. He's low showing, and triumphantly so.

Dave: (10♠) 4♥ 5♣ ~~Q~~♠ A♣
Q♦
Rodge: (?) ~~Q~~♥ 5♥ 7♥ 9♦
10♥

He knows my hand needed help and didn't get it, so he bets the limit, £10, as he should do. There's a cap of three raises per round but it's expensive to call.

I sit and mope at Rodge's hand. "Rodge, what've you got down there?" I put him on a pair of queens to begin with, so that would make his hand worse than mine, if he really has the case queen.

Trouble is, Rodge plays so erratically he could have anything, could even be an ace.

"Have you paired up, Rodge?" I go on.

"Why don't you stick your money in and find out?" Rodge inquires sweetly. "You're holding up the game!"

"All right, you're not such a bad guy, whatever your girl friends say," I answer. "I'll give you a call."

I call and cut the first raise to a pound, Flora takes the second £10 raise, of course, and Rodge caps it. So this round will cost me £31, which is absolutely stupid. Plus there is still another round of betting to come, after the declarations for high or low – what am I *doing* in this pot?

I should fold. But here's a funny thing. As Rodge puts in the final call and raise and counts his sheaf of pound notes down, he seems a touch too deliberate, as if demonstrating to me how much money is going in.

Something tells me all is not right with Rodge's hand.

Everyone has gone very quiet. I can't back out now, so I call the final bets.

We both show one coin in the hand, to declare low. Flora bets the final £20 and we both just call.

"What've you got?" Rodge asks.

"I saw *you*," I reply.

Rodge shows his hole card. It is the queen. His low is Q–10–9–7–5 against my Q–10–5–4–A.

I got it right, for once.

"You see I had to play it that way," Rodge starts explaining. "I knew you were high in the hole, so I had to go with it."

"You did the right thing, Rodge," I tell him.

And this time I mean it.

4

"I'm worried about Don," I tell Colin.

I'm calling from the office and don't particularly want anyone to overhear this side of my life.

"What are you worried about?" says Cool Colin, the mathematician in the game.

"He keeps on *losing*," I say. "You know £750 last week, £800 the week before. Can he afford it?"

"Why don't you ask him?" asks Colin.

Don is a salesman who doesn't make any sales and is always strapped for cash.

The bureau chief sticks his head over my desk: "You coming to the meeting, Dave?"

"Yeah, sure, I'll catch you upstairs." Into the phone I hiss: "I can't spend my whole day talking to you about cards! I'm holding a cheque from Don, that's all."

Why should it have to be me who holds his damn cheque is what I really want to know.

Colin's voice tails off. "See you tonight."

I scurry up to the office meeting which is about next year's budget. We're talking figures like phone numbers here, millions, and all I'm thinking about is a lousy cheque from Don for £750.

It's an amateur group, we've all played together for more years than we can remember. Maybe Don will have a winning night for a change.

"Hi, Don, howya doin?"

"Fine, fine!"

Don is a salesman, but exactly what he sells, if anything, is a mystery.

I take a seat next to him to give him moral support. I'm thinking about how's he's doing the whole time, so I can't concentrate. He wins a few early hands, then throws it all back.

"Loosen up will ya Dave?" booms Gerry.

"If I was any looser, you'd have to call the police," I tell him.

"Aw right, guys, the one you've all been waiting for, here it is! Big Cross."

Cries of enthusiasm and dismay greet this news. This is a

game where you have to make five cards, high or low, using a combination of any two cards from five cards dealt in your hand, plus any three from either line of a ten-card cross.

x
x
x x x x x
x
x

It's a weird game but we're a weird school. The loopier the hand, the better we like it.

The cards are turned face up two a time, with the middle card, which can count in either row of the cross, last.

I've got a playable hand A–2–2–3–10, looking for a low. First up cards on the cross are a 4 and a 5, which seem to help me, and then a 5 and a 4 which ruin me unless a 6 drops for a perfect 6–4 low.

"Dave!" sings out Colin. "Are we keeping you awake?"

"Sorry, just wondering if I'm ever going to get a hand."

"If you played a hand," growls Gerry, "you might catch something."

"I thought you caught something the other night," smirks Rodge.

"Now boys," says Flora, "let's stick to cards."

I'm stung into calling. Gerry raises and Colin re-raises.

Next card shows a 10 which gives me a pair for what it's worth. There's a lot of raising and re-raising. This is building into a big hand but there's too many straight and flush chances out to make my hand worth chasing. Even if a 6 falls I'll probably tie with another low and be quartered up.

So I fold. Maybe Don will manage to win a big one.

"What've you got?" I ask him.

We all peek at each other's hands when we're out of the pot, as a matter of course.

Don tips me his cards and I stare at them in amazement. He's raising like a bandit on absolutely nothing.

"Get my strategy?" Don says to me, in a saucy tone.

5♥
J♠
Cross: 4♥ 8♣ X 10♦ 5♦
Q♣
4♠

Don: A♠ 3♣ 4♣ 8♥ 9♦

"Go get 'em, baby!" I tell him.

I try to work out what he's up to. If he catches a 6 on the middle card of the cross he'll make a 6–5–4–3–A low, which is strictly second best. Someone is sure to have A–2 in their hand. Though as I folded two deuces, it does somewhat reduce the field.

Anyway, if a deuce flops as the centre card, he won't have a low at all but a five high straight.

If the centre card pairs another card in the cross, someone will almost certainly fill a high full house for the other half of the pot.

I go and pour a cup of coffee. I can't bear to watch him in self-destruct mode any longer.

The betting goes on at a furious pace. Then the middle card is turned over. It's the 6♠.

Colin bets like he's hit a lock 6–5–4 on the board with

an ace-deuce in his hand for low. The high hand has to be a spade flush.

But that doesn't deter Don. He calls all the raises, and pays another £10 for a change of card at the end. That's just to pep up the game, in case it ever gets boring.

There's no way Don can win it. But he goes on betting.

Out come the hands holding coins, one for low, two for high, three for both ways.

To my further astonishment Don has three coins in his hand. Now there's another round of betting. Colin looks distinctly queasy.

Don rolls over his cards.

"Nut high, nut low," he announces.

There's a moment of painful silence.

"Take it down," says Gerry.

"See, I caught the two of spades on the change," exults Don. And he picks up the card and kisses it. "Mm-mm, you beauty!"

"Take it easy Don!" admonishes Flora.

Don rakes in the pile of pound notes.

"Nice hand," I congratulate him.

"Nothing to it!" Don exults.

At the end of the night I corner him.

"Hey, Don, do you wanna pay off that cheque you gave me last week?"

"Yeah, sure. Well, actually, I can use the cash." Don is stuffing a sheaf of notes into his hip pocket. "Can you pay my cheque into the bank?"

"If you prefer it that way."

Don adds: "Just wait till the end of the month, will ya?"

"Fine, Don, fine."

5

Cows are grazing in the meadow, the air is balmy, the buds of May are rippling in the spring breeze like a sheaf of green £5 pound notes.

We are all in the country for a poker weekend.

"Goddammit, this is so good," announces Gerry, breaking open a new deck. "Getting away from the office for a weekend is better than a health cure."

"You don't do anything in the office except sit on your butt and ogle the secretaries," objects Rodge.

"Har, har."

"Okay," Ron inquires. "It's eleven a.m. How long we gonna play?" Ron, an antiques dealer, plays for value and likes to know what he's liable to get into.

"Till six. Break for lunch."

"Whaddaya mean?" demands Col, the mathematician. "We go right through till seven, take a break for dinner, and then play on tonight."

"I got seven seats reserved for the festival theatre tonight," says Flora.

"Whassat?" snorts Col.

"*Julius Caesar.*"

"Seen it before," smirks Rodge. "The butler did it."

"Let's see how we feel this evening, Flora-pops," suggests Col. "I mean we're here to play cards, right?"

"Lissen, I know a guy who'll give me returns at half price," says Ron. "Might as well take it. We can do the theatre back in town, any time."

"We can do the show," suggests Gerry, "if you like, 'n then come back and play all night."

I cut the deck to Rodge who announces his choice of game.

"Circle."

"It's too early for circle," Ron protests. "I don't like all these chancy games before the game has warmed up."

"This country air is so good," booms Gerry. "It'll wake you up."

"Might do if you stopped smoking."

"C'mon, we're wasting time," says Col. "We've only got the room for 48 hours."

Circle is one of those games we play, which is somewhere between fairly crazy and completely crazy but not quite as crazy as it looks. Eight cards are dealt in a circle and turned up two at a time. Players have to make a high or a low hand from two cards in their own five card hand and three *contiguous* cards in the circle.

It has a certain logic, but . . .

"Diddle in the middle!" adds Rodge.

"Oh no!" Col groans.

A final card – 'the diddle' – is turned up in the middle of the circle. If a player uses this card, he needs to use only two, instead of three, consecutive cards from the circle with it. Simple, hunh?

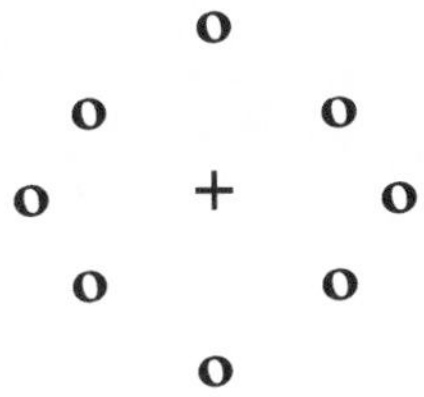

The first two cards turned north and south of the circle are a 2 and a 4. This already signals that a good low hand is very likely. I've got A–3–5 in my hand, with two high cards. Looks good, but without a 6 on board to go for the perfect 6-low, or at least a 7, I'm liable to be caught with a low straight. Everyone calls the opening round of bets.

The next two cards turned over are a jack and a queen. No visible improvement. Gerry now takes a raise, which is pretty obviously speculative. Four players call. Now it gets interesting because an ace turns. This is very bad news for me. It duplicates the ace I already have, and gives any other low cards hand missing an ace, like 2–3–6 or 2–4–6 a lot of help.

I hesitate. "Did the ace pair your low, sweetie?" Rodge inquires.

"I don't wanna win the first hand of the night, I mean the day," I flip back, folding.

Three players are left in and the last two up-cards of the circle are high, promising all sorts of straight and flush possibilities.

2♠

K♦ J♣

8♦ + A♠

Q♣ 10♥

4♥

Leaving aside the unkown 'diddle in the middle', the best low would be A–2–3–4–10 taking the three consecutive cards bottom right of the circle, where a player has 2–3 in his hand. What's second best low? Should be A–2–3–4–Jack, top right of the circle, with 3–4 in the hand.

No! A player might hold 2–5 to make A–2–4–5–10! This could easily stand up, depending on the diddle card. Tricky, but that's the kind of game it is.

On the high side, the A–J–10, middle right, make an obvious top straight if anyone has K-Q in their hand. And there are two flush draws, K–8 and 10–4, depending on the card in the middle.

There's a lot of betting by Gerry but Col comes along quietly – always an ominous sign. Ron drops.

Dealer turns over the diddle in the middle – A♦.

That does not change the best low but any pair signifies the possibility of a full house, in this case, A–A–J or A-A–10 on board if a player has the missing cards in his hand, say A–J or A–10, or a pair of jacks or tens. (In theory the high hand could be four aces, but I held an ace in my hand.)

Gerry bets it up, Col raises, Gerry re-raises, they go for their coins to declare.

Col sits and thinks, eyes popping through his specs, analysing the maths of it all. I think both of them have got a lock, high and low, but no – they both declare high. Gerry bets again, Colin thinks some more. He's got the maths all right, but not the discipline to fold with second best hand. He calls the final £40.

"Full house aces!" Gerry announces triumphantly. He turns over his five cards: A♥ K♠ Q♥ 9♠ 9♥.

Colin stares at his own cards. "You got me," he says. "Diamond flush."

"Hey, where's the house?" Ron inquires.

Gerry looks down. "Hell's buckets! I thought the third ace made it for me! I had the top straight going in, plus an ace-high flush draw as back-up. I was so sure I was best when the third ace came on the diddle, I completely misread my hand. I knew Col didn't have anything! God, what an idiot."

Colin spreads his diamond flush. He had read Gerry for nut low and had declared high, hoping to back in for half the pot. Instead he scoops the lot. (I note to my chagrin my 3–5 would have taken the low.)

"Bad luck, Gerry," Col says quietly, sweeping up a pile of pound notes.

One good rule in our game, which we stick to through thick and thin, is this: If you make a mistake in the final declaration, you do not whinge about it. You take it like a man.

Gerry finds a fat white envelope in his jacket and pulls out a wodge of red £50 notes.

"This country air," he snorts, "it's too damn fresh. Gimme a cigar."

6

"Family pot!" says Col, shuffling up.

"That'll be a nice change," says Gerry.

It's still early, the game is warming up, our little group of weekly addicts is looking to gamble.

I lean over to Col, who is the brainbox in the school.

"You're not gonna make us do higher mathematics again?"

"Everyone can play this one," responds Col in his dry way. "Even you, Dave."

"C'mon," says Flora. "put us out of our suspense!"

"Omaha high-low."

"Not enough betting, Col," booms Gerry.

"There will be this time. It's £10 to open."

"That's out of proportion," protests Ron, who is losing. "First bet is always £5."

"Same for everyone," Col says, holding the deck.

"There's a built-in advantage for the dealer," I complain.

"Statistically, yes," says Col. "Psychologically, no."

No one seems prepared to argue against this proposition.

"Hey, I gotta guy who can send over salt beef sandwiches and cucumber at £1.50 a throw," says Ron, who is a guy who likes a bargain.

No one evinces much enthusiasm for this offer.

"Plus coleslaw on the side, 60p."

"Play now, eat later," says Col.

Ron cuts and Col proceeds to deal.

"Hey wait a moment, is there an 8 or better qualifier for the low?" Flora asks.

"No!"

"Yes, there oughta be," says Ron. "Otherwise a hand like ace-deuce gets to bet the whole way."

"And what happens when another ace or a deuce flops?" inquires Col.

"Yeah, that's a point," Ron concedes.

"No qualifier, anything goes."

"Gotta use two cards in your hand, right?" asks Ron. The question has been asked a thousand times over the years.

"Solamente due," Roger confirms, in Italian.

I'm sitting one from last and find:

A♥ 4♦ 6♥ 7♣

Obviously a strongish hand, but as yet, no cigar. Everyone puts up their £10, which is way over the normal opening bet in this little school. But c'mon, we're here to play, guys!

The flop comes down:

A♦ 3♠ 9♥

This is annoying. I've got the makings of a good low or a straight for high, but it can so easily go wrong. I need a deuce for the nut low.

The betting now reverts to our usual progression. Ron kicks in with £5 and everyone calls.

The turn card is **5♥**.

Ron checks. Flora bets. "Let's try a little raise," says Gerry, "just one time." I see that anyone with a 2–4 is ruined for low because it makes a straight. 2–6 is good, but if Gerry had a lock he wouldn't have talked up his raise out loud, the way he did. Meanwhile I've got a draw for a nut flush high with a heart and a draw for a 9–high straight if an 8 comes down; plus a chance for the nut low, if a deuce comes on the river. As well as a second draw for the deuce, because after the flop is completed, we soup it up a bit by allowing a *change* of card. You have to think of all these things! Plus the fact that to soup it up a bit more, after the declarations, high or low, we have *another* round of betting.

So I call, as does Col. Five of us are left in to see the river card, which is **5♠**.

Now it's £10 to bet. Flora starts it. "Just one more time," says Gerry, raising again. Looks like the two fives on board have helped him. My two pairs aces and fives with a 7 kicker look weak. But I certainly can't fold for the money in the pot, so I call. And Col calls along.

Flora frowns at the flop, looks at her cards again. "Look at that," she says to Rodge, flashing her hand to him as she surrenders.

"I don't know how a girl of your incredible looks and IQ can resist," Rodge quips.

"Oh, I can resist anything," Flora remarks in her pert way, "well, almost anything."

I deduce from this exchange that Flora had a weak low, probably no deuce either.

Ron also folds: "Not wasting another dime on this one," he avers, getting up to tear a cold chicken apart and devour it in his fingers.

Now there's another round of betting and the three of us can change a card, cost £10. Gerry stands pat. Evidently he's made his hand. Got to be a full house fives, minimum.

Obviously I want to keep my 4♦ and 6♥ for the low. I think there's virtually no chance of catching another ace or 5 for a full house. But I keep the ace as emergency back-up and dump my 7 on the change. A miracle deuce might come, you never know. I can decide at the declaration if I should bail out with second best low hand. I toss in my tenner and peek at my change card. As fate would have it, another 7.

Flop A♦ 3♠ 9♥ 5♥ 5♠
Dave (A♥) 4♦ 6♥ ~~7♣~~
7♠

Col hesitates. "I'll dump that one," he says, placing £10

on top of his discard and sliding the change card off the deck.

"Are you sure you changed the right one?" I inquire.

"No need to be sarcastic," snaps Col.

"Psychic, hunh," says Gerry, counting down his cards, 1–2–3–4–5, like a reflex. He looks confident.

"Psychic-probabilistic," Col says, giving nothing away.

My hand, a minute ago so promising, has not improved. Without a deuce, I'm left with the second best low with this board, A–3–4–5–6.

I'm sure Gerry is high, with a full house. Col is just hanging in there to duck out the other way, as he always does when it comes down to three players. I have to call with my low.

We stick out our fists, I'm looking at Col, hoping he goes high. And he does so!

But Gerry, surprise surprise, is low. He didn't change a card, he must have the nut 2-6.

Now there's a final betting round. Gerry bets the £20. I call reluctantly and kill for a pound, Col raises and Gerry caps it, as he would anyway.

So it's £40 to me to see it through. Gerry can't be bluffing. The absolute best I can do, if he hasn't got a deuce, is to split the low half of the pot with him, which is a losing proposition. So I fold.

They rake in the money.

"What did you have for high, Col?" Gerry inquires as they cheerily divide the spoils.

Asking players about their hole cards is normal in our game, though it's not mandatory to tell the truth. But when someone pulls off a coup, the temptation is too great not to reveal it.

"Oh, just a couple of wee pairs," says Col, flipping his hand over.

I grimace.

"Anything wrong Dave?" Rodge inquires sweetly.

"No-o-o, I was well beaten," I fib bravely. My pathetic aces-up would have done the job.

"Where's the mayo?" calls Ron, rummaging in the fridge, mouth full of chicken.

"How did you know Gerry was going low, Col?" I ask him.

"Just bottom fishing!" snorts Gerry.

Col turns to me. "Didn't he raise when the pair of fives came down?"

"Oh yeah!" says Gerry. "Oh yeah. Oh yeah. Just keep trying that one, will ya?"

I grit my teeth.

7

We're short-handed tonight, so I call up Mel and get his current wife on the line.

"Hi, Joanie, it's Dave."

"Oh, hi." She does not sound too pleased to hear from me.

"Is Mel at home? Nothing special."

"I suppose you want to inveigle him into another of your poker games?" she says, frostily.

"No, Joanie. I mean well, yeah, we're getting a little game together tonight."

"Mel's on a sales call. And he can't play cards, anyway. We're going out this evening."

"Okay Joanie, thanks. Er, nice talkin' to ya," I hang up.

We really need Mel to make up the numbers, so this is a blow. We'll just have to play short-handed.

So when Mel showed up at the game on time, the guys were pleasantly surprised.

"You made the sale?" I greeted him.

"Yeah," says Mel, "but do me a favour, will ya? Don't call me at home."

Mel is a real estate operator, with a special talent for wrecking his own household.

"Sorry, Mel-baby."

"Joanie has a sort of hang-up about cards. Thinks I'm wasting my time."

"Wha-a-a-t!" booms Gerry, waving a nine-inch cigar. "This is the most stimulating, intellectual, high-minded group of guys in the country. A night spent down here is as good as a liberal education."

"Better," says Col, breaking open a new deck.

"She sounded okay on the phone, Mel," I lie.

"Yeah? First time I've known her sound okay for a month."

"Aw right, first one-eyed jack for dealer," says Col, always keen to get on with it.

A couple of hours in, we're midway through a hand of seven card high-low, when the phone rings.

This is a tricky hand. I've been dealt, luckily enough, 6s wired. We roll each card, face up or down, so I want to turn up low cards, to get everyone going the wrong way.

And amazingly, I manage to do just that. On sixth street, I show:

(6♠ 6♦) 6♣ 5♥ 4♠ 3♣

This is a great-looking hand. I suspect that Gerry has aces up, maybe trip fours. He's showing:

(x x) 4♦ A♠ 4♥ J♠

If I can only pair up, I'll murder him.

Gerry picks up the phone.

"Yup," he says curtly.

He passes the phone over to Mel.

"Oh hi, Joan," Mel responds, without enthusiasm.

"A noise in the basement? Gee, well it's probably the boiler, hon. You know." He hisses to me: "What's the bet?"

"Ten and raise ten", I tell him. Mel calls, still talking. Gerry re-raises and I take the last raise.

Mel is sitting on A♣ 7♥ 5♠ 6♥ which looks very good for low but he can't bet into my low. I'm sure he hasn't got better than a rough 8. He turned the ace first card, which implies bad starting cards in the hole. Three fours have gone for sure, and I've seen two threes and two deuces on hands which folded. So how can he improve?

Mel is still holding the phone. "Yeah, of course I can drive back, hon, if you need me. We're finishing about midnight, anyway." He rolls his eyes up to the ceiling.

Now comes the last down-card. I catch a 2♥ which makes me a low straight, which is completely useless. Probably can't beat Gerry for the high and I've got no low at all. The wheel doesn't work. In this game the nut low is A–2–3–4–6, with straights and flushes counting high only.

My board looks great though. Somehow, I've got to make Mel fold his eight or maybe rough seven low.

Gerry is high and bets £10. I raise, and Mel calls without even looking at the cards.

"What sort of noise?" he asks. "Okay, hon, you know me. Always ready to deal with things that go bump in the night."

Gerry takes the second raise. I can't back out now, so I cap it.

"Yeah, yeah. I'll be right over." Mel hangs up. "*Shee-it*," he says.

"Just £20," I tell him, lightly, trying to give the impression I want him to call my made 6.

At last Mel takes a look at our up-cards side by side.

Mel: (x x) A♣ 7♥ 5♠ 6♥ (x)
Dave: (x x) 6♣ 5♥ 4♠ 3♣ (x)

"Well, I gotta go, anyways," he says. "Might as well call!"

There's still a change card to come. £5 to exchange an up-card and £10 for a card in the hole. I don't know what to do. With so many low cards out there's no way I'm going to catch a pair to pump up my trip sixes. Is it worth paying £10 for the case ace to make a 6–low, or a 7 for a 7–5 low, which are the only cards which will help me? I figure it's much smarter to persuade Mel I've got an ace already, sitting on a lock.

"No change for me!" I tell Col, who is dealing this one. "Can't afford it."

"Hunh," Mel grunts, studying his hole cards. "I'll invest a fiver." He flips the 7 away from his up-cards. That almost certainly means he has another 7 duplicated in the hole. He changes the up-card because it's £5 cheaper than taking it down.

Mel gets an 8♦.

Gerry stands pat. He's obviously got his boat and sees no need to pay to change a card just for deception.

There's another round of betting, which goes all the way and we declare.

At the crucial moment, the phone rings again. Mel snatches it up.

"YEAH?" he yells. He listens. "JUST LEAVIN'!" He bawls, like a toastmaster announcing the departure of royalty. He listens some more. "Sure, a carton of milk, okay."

I don't believe my straight can possibly stand up for high. Mel and I both call low.

In this game, we have another round of betting, after the declarations. Crazy, but that's the way it is. I've got one last chance to shake Mel out of it.

"You gotta go, Mel?" I inquire sympathetically. "Too bad."

He doesn't answer me.

Gerry bets the statutory £20 and I raise it to £40. "Why don't you go now, Mel? You'll save money anyway," I tell him, as if the hand is all over.

Instead, he shoves in another £20 raise. "What the hell difference!" he says savagely.

Gerry caps it, naturally, but I can't even call.

"Nice play, Mel," I tell him, folding. "I think you just got me." He obviously smelt my straight.

"I had a 7," he says, doing me the courtesy of showing his hole cards, which he did not need to do.

"Good hand," I tell him. "Did you have the full, Gerry?"

"Only trip 4s," he says. But as he buries his hand in the deck I'll never know. I feel lower than a rat's arse.

Mel stuffs a wodge of pound notes in his pocket and zips up his parka, turns at the door:

"A man's gotta do what a man's gotta do," he says.

8

Last hand of the night we double the bets. What is known among racing men as the 'Get out of trouble stakes'.

In this regular weekly joust between a bunch of guys, and one gal, who have all played with each other for yonks, the betting starts at £3 and goes up to £20 a round with three raises. You can win or lose £1,000 on the night, but no one is going to break the bank.

In this final hand it's double stakes, which means double joy – or double trouble.

"Which way are you going, Dave sweetie?" inquires Rodge facetiously.

"I am still studying the manifold possibilities," I tell him.

"Just want you to get it right," he says.

We're playing a game called Elevator, which I'll try and explain in a moment.

After a lot of betting and raising, I've managed to drive everybody out but Rodge and Flora. I'm sitting on a near perfect low hand. I don't want either of them calling with the same nut low, to split the low side, so reducing my share to a quarter of the pot.

Rodge bets, I raise, and Flora who is quite a fast little number, well able to give as good as she gets with these guys, is hesitating. She peeks down at her cards.

"Flora," says Rodge, "as one of your greatest admirers, I advise you to get your sweet bippy out of it. Sorry! I mean withdraw gracefully."

"After that charming piece of advice," Flora says, "what is a girl to do? I fold!"

"I suppose you're looking for a split?" I ask Rodge, fishing.

Rodge and I are the only two left in the pot, and we do allow making deals in this sort of situation.

"No-o-o thanks," says Rodge. "Not this one, sweetie. Raise again!"

Rodge is a tax exile, with a good line in patter and three ex-wives scattered around the country to prove it.

I call his bet. "Rodge," I counter, "you are liable to wind up a very sick bunny."

I'm pretty sure I've got him beat for the low but the elevator card is still to be turned over.

"Oh, I'm a pretty sick bunny already," says Rodge cheerfully. "One hand more won't make any difference."

I know Rodge is up to something but I'm not sure what. He's an irredeemable gambler, who always chases his luck when he's losing, like tonight. I'm worried about his going high-low. The risk if you declare high-low is you've got to *win* both ways. Lose one way, you forfeit the other, even if you are perfect. So everyone is fairly wary about it.

In Elevator, eight cards are dealt face down in the middle, in two lines of four, and then turned up two at a time. A player has to use two cards from the board, crosswise, plus three cards from his own hand of five cards to make a high or a low; or three cards from the board, crosswise, including the elevator card, plus two from his hand.

x x
x x
e
x x
x x

The card in the middle, which is turned up last, is the elevator. It can move up or down between the two lines of four cards so as to be combined with either or both of the two cards on either side of it.

What could be simpler than that?

I'm sitting on a low hand, A–2–3–7–K which is good but only second best. The A–2–3 make a 7–6 low, with the bottom line of cards on the board shown below. The 2 and 7 on the top line of the board don't help me because they are duplicated in my hand.

7♥ 2♠
J♠ 5♠
e
10♦ 8♣
7♣ 6♥
Dave: A♣ 2♦ 3♦ 7♠ K♠

But if Rodge happens to have A–3–4 in his hand, he's got me beat on the top line with a royal 7. Rodge is the kind of player who when he's chasing will try and make spaghetti stand up. But from the way he's talked his way through the hand, I'm pretty sure he's on a draw to hit it.

Anyway, I can't back out now. The elevator card is turned over and it's a 4♠. That is great news for me. It gives me the nut low A–2–3 plus the elevator card 4 and the 6 in the bottom line of the up-cards. If Rodge has A–3–4 in his hand as I suspected, or A–2–4 or A–2–5, he's out of it.

There's another round of betting. I don't want to go mad. If there's any chance of a coup it lies in persuading Rodge that, really, I've got the nut high hand, so he should declare low with second best to save half the pot. Then I scoop. But there's nothing out on the high side, like a pair showing, to make another raise by me seem convincing.

It looks as if the best high hand either of us can make is a spade flush (though concealed full houses are always possible in this game). I've got the K♠ 3♠ with J♠ 4♠ 5♠ on board, but I'm frightened of the ace of spades. Rodge has certainly got an ace – why not the A♠? Although he may not have another spade to go with it, a high call is too risky.

So when he raises my bet, I just call along. You never know, he might get greedy . . .

I hold one coin in my hand for low, and as I hoped, Rodge shows three coins, for both ways. He's unopposed for the high and he must surely have a lock low. He's going to get three-quarters of this monster pot, dammit, leaving me with a quarter from splitting the low half.

"I've got the A–3–6, sweetie," Rodge announces. The 2 on the top line plus the elevator card makes the nut low.

It's a red ace, I see.

"Yeah," I say grudgingly, showing my A–2–3. "What was your high? Top flush?"

"Good golly, Miss Molly, what d'ya think I play on, Dave? All I got's an itsy-bitsy little 7–high straight."

"Weren't you worried you'd lose the whole pot?" I ask, biting back my annoyance. "Any flush beats you."

"A flush?" Rodge inquires innocently. "Is there a flush out there? Didn't even cross my tiny mind."

He starts hauling in the pot. "Three-quarters for me, a quarter for you, sweetie. Do you want to cut it up?"

"Why don't you do it, Rodge," I tell him. "You're the happy bunny."

And the game rocks on, week after week. We all act like overgrown schoolboys, the poker is a bit silly – granted. But in a way these nights mark a high point of the week.

5

Net Poker

The virtual casino is the equivalent to placing a slot machine in millions of homes.

Anthony Cabot and Kevin Doty

In the modern world, you don't even need to round up other players to get a poker game. They can be located, day or night, on the net.

I clicked on the Internet (my new toy) and told it to search for 'poker'. It listed 31,100 entries. Dedicated to the game as I am, I wasn't sure I could surf through quite so many items, even in a year's research. So I consulted one or two friends on how to get into the subject.

There are several ways in. One is via the *www.ConJelCo.com* web site. This is a gambling books and software publishing company specialising in products for serious gamblers. "In addition we offer high quality books, newsletters, software, and videos on blackjack, craps, video poker, and general gambling topics from the publishers," states their blurb. The excellent ConJelCo service also provides a blow-by-blow account of each successive event in the World Series of Poker.[1]

This is (or was) a labour of love performed by Tom Sims, a veteran recorder of poker news, living in Las Vegas. He and his team did this job, which also has a certain historic value, to promote the bookselling operation.

Then I went the European route. I tried *http://eppa.bigfoot.com* which also did the trick. Up came a series of buttons listing various topics on the web site run by the pioneering European Poker Players' Association. I began with the News Update button. This gave the tournament schedule in Europe. Then I got the European poker rankings, rather like the international tennis rankings, as compiled by the EPPA. (I should add that as the world's most untechnically-minded person, who can hardly screw in a light bulb without fusing the entire house, getting on the net was no small achievement.)

Recording world championship hands is not as easy as it sounds. Sims would dictate a play-by-play description of each hand into a microcassette recorder and when the game was over for the night, rush off home to transcribe his running commentary in time for breakfast hackers on the ConJelco website. "Poker on the net will never replace books," Sims told me – which is reassuring to those of us non-computer nerds who have been brought up on the printed word.

Sims could evidently play poker a bit on his own account. He defeated 112 opponents to take first place in

[1] In the latter years of the World Series up to 1998.

the BARGE pot limit Hold 'em event in 1995. BARGE stands for Big August Rec.Gambling Excursion, which is a get together in Vegas of people who meet electronically on the Internet news group *Rec.Gambling Poker* (accessible via *ConJelCo.com*). This news group is a running bulletin board for poker players who want to exchange ideas, debate current issues or seek advice. It can be silly and serious, hilarious or instructive, and represents an extraordinary kind of free-for-all dialogue, averaging scores of new messages a day.

Most of them are fairly inconsequential, seeking information about poker games or commenting on hands, one or two are more serious. Overall the net effect (so to speak) is to bring poker players together via a daily bulletin board, for those who want to feel a sense of community with their fellow players. I like this one, taken at random:

"A stockbroker that I regularly play poker against said that if one of his clients asks about investing in commodity futures, he asks him to take a $100 bill out of his wallet and burn it. If the man baulks at this advice, he tells him to make other investments."

Sims now spends a fair amount of time on poker machines – it takes even an expert slots player about 100 hours to work (not play!) through 40,000 hands, which is the expected frequency of a royal straight flush. He claims that by correct play on the quarter machines, deuces wild, he has achieved an edge of 1.6%. This is indeed a fabulous return, better than the best blackjack counters can achieve.

Why do casinos allow it? As with blackjack, which is a beatable game, casinos encourage players who believe, in theory, they can win. In practice very few gamblers can play the machine absolutely correctly based on perfect computer odds on every hand dealt. The serious profit comes from hitting royal straight flushes. If you want to play these machines, which are fun for half an hour before dinner, that is what you must aim for. "I've done it a whole bunch of times," Sims says. "As for the comps from the casino, I could eat for nothing for the rest of my life."

The Rec.Gambling weekend, hosted by Binion's (who at that time saw an interest in getting online with poker players) is a frivolous affair, when computer nerds take their fingers off the keyboard and click on to real life. It includes among all the celebration drinks and dinners the world Roshambo championship (i.e. rock, paper, scissors). Other groups are springing up around the country in places like Foxwoods and Atlantic City.

Yet another way into the net is via the Las Vegas pair of authors David Sklansky and Mason Malmuth. Apart from their series of books, published under the Two Plus Two imprint, they offer various gambling essays on screen at *twoplustwo.com*, and challenging items like a poker quiz.

What I wanted to try, first of all, was actually playing poker for money (via credit card) on the net. I knew that this was on offer for casino gambling. Could it possibly work for poker? It would seem at first glance to be a very risky business.

I went down to the city office of a poker-playing friend, who occasionally lightened his business duties with an interlude of virtual poker. Laurence had registered his name and credit card details with an outfit called Planet Online Services. This organisation was run from Duluth, Georgia, but the poker was played in Costa Rica because, as everyone knows, gambling across state lines in the US is illegal. Laurence had accepted, according to the draft authorisation he had signed, that it was his responsibility, if applicable, to report financial information to his government, customs or tax jurisdiction.

Planet Poker explained its service at some length. It described itself as an internet gaming company dedicated to providing customers with a legal electronic venue to play poker on the Internet. "Planet Poker's mission is to provide individuals with a complete card room experience, the excitement of a trip to your local card room without leaving your home."

So after Laurence logged on, a picture of the outside of a casino card room came up on the screen. The doors opened and there we were – inside the card room with none of the problems of driving in and parking and waiting for a seat. It was now 12 noon on a sunny London morning, 4 a.m. in California.

Five players were engaged in a game of Hold 'em. They had their own cyberspace names – Baddog, Scooter, Painter Pat, Buster. Laurence knew them from playing in previous games – 'knew them', that is, by their style of play. The game was $10–$20 limit Hold 'em, played quite fast, as you would expect from electronic simulation of the deal and betting. After each hand, the result was given and the player's running total of wins or losses was shown.

In a basic $3–$6 game, Planet Poker took 5% of each pot as its rake, kicking in at $1 for a $20 pot, increasing to $2 when the pot size reached $40 and capping at $3 for pots over $60, just like in a regular casino. But it took no part in the game as such. The speed of play would yield it something like $90 an hour in such a game. The same rake applied in the $5–$10 and $10–$20 games.

The company claimed it had designed its services "for providing excitement and entertainment to individuals around the world". It was entirely in the company's own interest, it assured potential punters, to protect the integrity of the game and assure its customers' confidence. "All winnings go to the players. Once winnings have been transferred from the game to your player's account you can keep it in your account to play again or be reimbursed via wire transfer or cheque."

In a series of answers to frequently asked questions, Planet Poker cited this desperate inquiry: *"A table seized up and all my money is GONE! What do I do?"*

Answer: "When a table locks up for whatever reason (we're working on this one!) your money is locked in the database. It isn't gone so don't panic. In order to release your money, you should try and return to the table that locked up. If the 'lockup' was temporary, then your money will be released to you once you sit down. If the 'lockup' is more serious then you should page a Planet Poker operator. They will come to the tables and reset the games. This usually involves a five-minute interruption in the game play for everyone, but once the tables have been reset, all money locked in the database is released to the player's account."

Another frequently asked question was: "How do I chat with other players?" (Chat is an important aspect of poker games.) Answer: "To chat with other players, simply begin typing while on the tables. A box will open to show your message, press enter and your message will be seen by other players."

"How do I collect my winnings?" "Any winnings you wish to cash out will be sent via cheque to you. To request a cash out, e-mail Planet Poker." One player who lost $96 out of his hundred requested payment of his remaining four bucks. He was surprised to find the address on the handwritten cheque was from Nevada, the return address on the envelope was in Florida and the postmark was from Canada! And the company is supposedly located in Costa Rica.

Laurence was in ebullient mood. He had recently e-mailed a request to be paid his winnings on previous jousts, and a cheque had arrived within the week. This morning, to show me the ropes, he played a couple of hands at blackjack, and won $25. Well, as they say of journalism, it's better than working.

Another company, Virtual Vegas, offered some interesting figures for casino spending on the net. Based in Santa Monica, Virtual Vegas was launched in 1994, offering free games with prizes, and not (for legal reasons) on-line wagering. According to an interview with its founder David Herschman, in Internet Gaming International's newsletter (January 8, 1998) Virtual Vegas was the first online casino and was popular right from the start.

They could have made more money by running a virtual casino, offshore, Herschman explained, but their strategy was different. He has a twenty-year business plan, to become a virtual city – a cyberspace replica of Las Vegas – "a place for people to come, meet their friends, chat, shop, play games, do whatever they need to do entertainment-wise . . . We're really here to service the sponsors." Sponsors are charged a flat rate for banners of $50 per thousand subscribers.

They could get 20 times more people to come and play for free than to play for real money, Herschman added, and by doing that, he could build a significant brand. The brand name is crucial. "Maybe there will be 100 casinos by the end of the year, of which maybe five will be building any significant business and be potential $100m. companies."

So how much does each player spend on average? "$150 to $1,000 loss per month per player. That's just information I get from our sponsors. I see that definitely as a downward trend . . . I think that number will eventually settle to the $50 to $100 range within the next five years."

Herschman's target is to get over a million regular players in the next couple of years, and then figure out what he can do, legally, with these customers.

The legal issue is paramount, because – as everyone can see – gambling already exists in cyberspace. Gambling on the net is referred to as *nambling*. The word cyberspace comes from a 1984 novel by William Gibson called *Neuromancer*, which describes a three-dimensional electronic representation of the real world where the characters interact. As explained by Cabot and Doty in their paper on Internet Gambling[2]: "The technical world adopted the term to mean all media used to transmit information, either digitally or electronically."

Among these, the most widely used service is the Internet which, as we all know, is a network of networks of millions of computers across the world. The person calling can be in the same country or different countries; be next

[2] *Internet Gambling: Jurisdiction Problems and the Role of Federal Law, Gaming Law Review*, volume 1, number 1, 1997, Anthony N. Cabot and Kevin D. Doty

door to each other or thousands of miles away. A virtual casino, therefore, can be based in one country, while the casino patrons come from every other part of the globe. The problem, from the legal point of view, is that people can easily access online gambling, if they choose to do so, regardless of official policy.

Take a state like Utah, where the legislature decides that gambling in any form is unacceptable – either on moral grounds ("God says that gambling is wrong") or for practical reasons (the social problems). If citizens of Utah gamble at home via a virtual casino they clearly frustrate public policy.

But what about Nevada where gambling is legal? – though taxed and regulated. "Who regulates gambling on the Internet to ensure that the games are honest?" the authors ask. "Who licenses the operation and assures that they have sufficient bankrolls to pay winning wagers? Who resolves disputes that the patrons may have with the casino? What prevents the casino from closing down and taking all the money in the patrons' accounts?"

The answer to all these questions is: "No one and nothing." The credibility of the gambling industry, they conclude, is left in the hands of every shyster, wiseguy or con artist who can afford a computer and a programmer. (The point was underlined at an Emerging Crime conference in London in March 1999, which was warned that Internet gamblers were being targeted by crime gangs who set up virtual casinos.)

"The games can be rigged, winnings may not be paid, and by giving casinos their credit card details, net gamblers could be jeopardising their financial security." There were further fears that children could gamble away the family fortune. Any child with access to their parents' credit cards could gamble on the net, as it is impossible to check a player's age or identity. (Might the 'home alone' kids win? Subversive thought!)

Similarly in Britain, the newly appointed Chairman of the Gaming Board, Peter Dean, noted that an Internet casino operation could not lawfully be established. Casino gaming can only be conducted on licensed premises, and the players must under the legislation be physically present on the premises. But there is nothing in law to prevent a player resident in Britain gambling on an Internet casino established abroad.

I think one might put it the other way round. There is nothing governments can do to stop players' access to casinos via their computers if they choose to log on. That is the real power of freedom of communication via cyberspace (which, quite apart from gambling, is making an enormous impact on politics and freedom of expression all over the world).

In Nevada, where the overall objective of politicians and regulators is – not surprisingly – to protect the casino industry, online bets are against the law. A Nevada Revised Statute forbids placing wagers via mail, telephone, television, cable, wire, facsimile and the Internet. The Internet was added to the list during the 1997 legislative session.

Nevada is the first state explicitly to prohibit – and allow – gambling via the Internet. Professor Nelson Rose, a leading authority on gambling and the law, summed up the situation as follows: An Internet operator, anywhere in the world, who accepts a wager from a person who is physically present in Nevada is committing a misdemeanour and "may be prosecuted within this state".

Anyone who makes a bet from Nevada via the Internet is committing a misdemeanour, regardless of where the person accepting the wager may be.

This is the first, and so far only, law in America, Rose noted, which makes it a crime to make a bet on the Internet. Servers (i.e. providers of Internet facilities) are also now covered, if they are aware gambling is taking place. It is a crime to "knowingly . . . send, transmit or relay" a wager from within Nevada to anywhere via the Internet, or from outside the state into Nevada via the Internet.

Because this is Nevada, Rose pointed out, it should come as no surprise that the new criminal penalties do not apply to wagers accepted in the state by Nevada-licensed race and sports books; Nevada-licensed off-track and pari-mutuel betting operators; and "any other person or establishment that is licensed to engage in wagering in Nevada" – meaning casinos. Notice it is a crime for a Nevada resident to make an out of state bet, but perfectly legal for Nevada operators to accept wagers from anywhere in the world, Rose added (Draft paper on the Law of Internet Gambling, 1999).

Would Nevada residents get into trouble for placing a bet at an Internet casino? "That's the difficult part," admitted Jeff Rodefer, Deputy Attorney General in Nevada's gaming division. "The Gaming Control Board doesn't have the people to police the Internet and find out if Citizen Q is placing a bet from her home. They're grappling not so much with it being illegal as how to enforce it."

Quite so; but could one imagine some diabolical electronic device being invented which could retrace and record citizens' calls on the net? In this Orwellian world, quite probably.

A curious instance of exposure came up recently when a report of a businessman's high stakes poker play suddenly appeared on the net. It badly upset both the player and the Bellagio card room where the action occurred. A journalist, watching the game from the rail, chose to file a report describing the series of $50,000 bets this player was making. His bank, located in another country, which had a number of loans out to him, somehow got to see the report, and was extremely upset, though not half as upset as the management of the casino, at this betrayal of a customer's privacy.

And what if such a report were entirely fictitious? The net can be a dangerous medium.

One country which has had Internet betting (via licensed bookmakers in the Northern Territory) since 1996 is Australia. The punters certainly know it's there. They've been extraordinarily successful in attracting bets from all over the world, Professor Jan McMillen, Executive Director of the Australian Institute for Gambling Research, told me.

Unlike the US, the Australian state governments consider Internet/interactive gaming as e-commerce – i.e. not a special case. Another difference from the US is that gambling is the constitutional domain of the states; the federal government has no role. (New Zealand drafted legislation in 1997 but it stalled at the Cabinet level.)

The general approach to Internet gaming in Australia is that prohibition is impossible, so the preferred option is to regulate to the highest standards achievable. There is not uniform support for this, nor is there agreement about the regulatory framework.

In 1997 the state regulators developed a 'national model'

which outlined the minimum standards and procedures for Internet/interactive gaming regulation. Most states have publicly endorsed this national approach, but one or two have yet to do so.

Australian governments are aware of developments in the US and anticipate commercial, political and legal attempts to restrict Australian Internet operations. Australians have had similar disputes with 'our friends across the Pacific' for many years – it's accepted as part of life in a global economy.

As expected, when the National Gambling Impact Study Commission published its report in May 1999, it recommended federal prohibition of Internet gambling within the United States. It requested the Department of Justice to develop "enforcement strategies" covering Internet service providers, credit card companies and money transfer agencies.

In a withering condemnation of the whole report, Nelson Rose said the report was so lightweight you would have to put a brick on it to stop it floating away. The reason they sought a ban on Internet gambling, he suggested, was that it was – like a common enemy – the one thing that supporters of casino gambling and the opponents of gambling could agree on. "Since it may be technologically impossible to completely block the Internet, banning Internet gambling may be like trying to stop the wind."

For my first trial at poker on the net, I put $200 (of Laurence's money) on the table. There were five other players in the game, which was $3–$6 limit-raise Hold 'em, the basic casino game, with blinds of $1 and $3. Judging from their locations given alongside their names, they were from California, but they included one Alico from Istanbul.

First hand, when I had to post, (put up the blind of $3) I found (7–7) in the hole and got three callers. The button (which is the buck moving around after each hand to show the order of betting) and the other players' action, were all very clearly shown on screen. Three callers. The flop came down 2–3–10 with two hearts. I bet to test the opposition and got one caller. On the next card I checked, he bet and I folded. Laurence was miffed at my timidity.

My third hand I found A–7 off-suit and raised. No help from the flop. Check, check, and Sager from San Jose won on a pair of jacks. So I was right not to push it that time. Before each deal, the noise of a shuffle was played out from the screen, replicating 'real' poker. The hands moved around pretty fast, with only four or five players involved (sometimes people sat out). After a succession of losses, I found myself down $28.

Then I found A-Q clubs in the hole and raised, just one caller. The flop was no help, I bet again, and then again on fourth street. On the river a three came down, pairing the turn card. I would have checked but Laurence egged me on to give it a shot. I bet the $6 and my opponent folded! After 15 minutes and twelve hands I was $1 ahead.

Time to chat. I started by typing a message to Alico in Istanbul. "Are you still there?" "Yep." "How is life?" "So-so." "Are there casinos in Turkey?" "They are closed. By law." "Do you enjoy playing on the net?" (All this was going on during the play. Alico's mood must have been improved by hitting a full house.) Answer: "Very much."

Then I asked Copperfeld from Burnaby where he was

from. British Columbia. He was playing poker on the net for a new experience. He had played for two days. What? He meant two sessions in two days. *Lol* – computer acronym for laugh out loud.

I signed off to go to lunch. I found the experience of playing on the net quite amusing. It seemed tailor-made for people who are lonely or cut off from a proper card game. Why not? It passes the time and you might win a little and at these stakes, the downside risk was very low. The main problem was when a blip in the software interfered with the connexion. If you were booted off when holding a full house, it would be a bit discouraging.

Richard, another poker-playing friend explained: "When you live in the depths of the country, as I do, and there is no poker game within easy reach, the net is better than nothing. Of course it's a complete distortion of the real game. You can't shift people by betting at them, because they're playing 'no fold 'em, hold 'em'."

Richard would play an hour or two at a time, but some people went in for eight or ten-hour sessions. For Americans, he pointed out, all local calls are free, so they can log on to the net at zero cost.

Caveat emptor! Let the buyer beware, as the lawyers advise. No matter how fulsome the protestations of the organisers about their own probity, players are bound to be wary of such games, played in cyberspace.

For example, two players might be able to collude, by sending each other private messages about their hole cards. Other players in the game would know nothing about it. With say, 300 players registering to play, there would be an obvious temptation for 'teams' to get together. Whether the operating staff would be sufficiently skilled to identify patterns of team play is an open question. Would they even be interested in looking? The company running a virtual poker makes its money by the rake, on every hand.

After a time Laurence began to suspect something funny might be going on. Nothing you could really put your finger on and say – "that's fixed!" Just a sense, as you might get in a regular poker game, that a couple of players were working together and that you were the pig in the middle. People betting at you in weird situations. For instance, a player who had been leading the betting might then fold at the end after checking, leaving the other player involved in the hand to take the pot. Laurence felt uneasy about the \$10–\$20 game. Certainly if two players were in collusion, by signalling each other their hands, they could clean up. The lower level games he felt were safe enough.

His impression of collusion was strongly reinforced by a warning from a contributor on the net who reported that it was *definitely* going on in the \$10–\$20 game. "The question is, therefore, should we talk openly about it or should we pretend it isn't happening?"

A message I picked up on the net asked what was to stop two players being on a telephone link discussing each hand and 'working' the game? Nothing at all, was the answer. Or they could 'instant message' each other, or one person could have a couple of lines, modems and computers and play both hands himself. As you can never prove these things, the only solution, it seems to me, is to stop playing.

Richard, who admits he is a poor limit-game player, lost \$300 over 10–12 hours' play. He did the worst damage in three-hour games, which is quite a long time to gaze at the computer screen and hold your concentration. Small stuff – "We pay for our pleasures in life in a multitude of ways," opined Richard sagely. As for myself, I am not sure I want to send out my credit card details across the ether to operators I don't know. Players can also deposit a cheque but a 6% service charge is levied on each transaction.

Speaking of cheating, one of the more literate contributors to the net noted that there was a deep philosophical divide between the absolutely ethical person, who would say "I will not cheat in any circumstances" and the 'situational ethic' of the person who would say "I will not cheat unless it is necessary to obtain some greater good." (In this case, winning at a poker game.) The writer commented that there were two fundamental and incompatible methods of reasoning about moral issues: reasoning from principles and reasoning from consequences. Philosophers and theologians had been arguing this one for centuries without reaching any real conclusion. In their daily life, he added, people tended to switch between both methods.

I asked Stanford Wong, the noted authority on blackjack, how he assessed blackjack on the net. "I am leery of gambling on the Internet," he told me. "If a customer experiences a problem with an Internet casino, the customer has too little recourse for solving that problem. I have heard accounts of customers getting screwed by Internet casinos, and being unable to do anything about it. There is no mechanism that forces an Internet casino to be honest." If and when that day came, Wong added, he would start covering Internet casinos in his publications.

The same problem arose with Indian casinos, Wong added. "Indians hide behind their sovereignty in disputes with their casino customers, with the result that customers sometimes get screwed and there is nothing they can do about it. No law enforcement agency has jurisdiction, and nobody can sue an Indian tribe unless the tribe allows itself to be sued, which just does not happen."

Nelson Rose summed up these questions about probity: Can the operator be trusted? Is the game honest? Is the financial transaction secure? Has the operator got connections with organised crime? Further, can the law minimise lost work and school time, protect players from themselves, especially problem gamblers and minors? Are criminal laws being broken – by the bettor? operator? server? financier? site developer?

Just how tricky it all is was shown by a flaw in the algorithm (process of calculation) later discovered in Planet Poker's method of dealing out the cards on screen. This was not the result of a hacker trying to cheat, but the work of serious programmers, testing a tricky mathematical conundrum. Generating a random shuffling routine on a computer is a very complicated process. A company called RST Corp cracked the algorithm from the source code, which Planet Poker had published to demonstrate it was fair.

The flaw came in the shuffle, which stemmed from the seemingly abstruse figure of the number of milliseconds elapsed since midnight. You might think this was enough to baffle anybody. But you would be wrong.

The shuffling algorithm always started with an ordered deck of cards and then generated a sequence of random numbers to reorder the deck. For technical reasons, the algorithm could produce only slightly more than 4 billion possible decks of cards, a number much smaller than the 52 factorial combinations possible in a real deck of cards.

"To make matters worse," a correspondent on the news group noted, "the algorithm chose a seed based on the number of milliseconds since midnight." Since there are only 86,400,000 milliseconds in a day, the number of possible decks was now reduced to this figure – "an astonishing magnitude of loss of possible hands which can be dealt".

The programmers publicised their findings – the incident even attracted notice on TV and in the press. Planet Poker, which claimed it had discovered the flaw for itself, changed its algorithm, to show it was aware of the problems and give the players a sense of confidence. "We have worked very hard to establish our reputation as an honest card room. We continue to work to keep that reputation." Even so, the computer whizzes were not entirely convinced. They wanted to test the new code for themselves. Planet Poker also hired Mike Caro, the self-styled 'mad genius of poker', as a consultant.

Another way of practising poker is via computer games (as distinct from nambling). One of the best is *World Championship*, which simulates, quite precisely, the cycle of the event – satellites, the opening rounds, the progressive jumps to higher blinds and antes, right up to the final table, if you can get that far.

First of all a figure resembling Jack Binion appears on the screen, pronouncing the time-honoured command to 'Shuffle up and deal', alongside tournament director Jack McClellan. (These veterans of the world championship, alas, disappeared from the event in 1999.) So the player finds himself with $10,000 worth of chips at one of the 24 tables set up for the event.

The 'play' is fast and easy to control. Simply clicking on a little window marked 'check, bet or raise' when it comes round to your turn. The play moves around the table, with players posting small and big blinds in turn, with each participant's total value of chips shown by his seat. In one way, as the antes and blinds increase at regular intervals, this game offers a good model, like a training exercise, for the world championship itself.

Its drawback, so it seemed to me, was that the *character* of the different players was not conveyed, so there was no way of gauging an opponent's strength or style, beyond noting his total amount of chips. The best way to play, it seemed, was to follow Hold 'em values (see Appendix, page 241) and bet accordingly. One realistic point was that big or all-in bets seemed to be respected by opponents.

When you 'win' the world championship, by eliminating all the other players, as my friend George did on two occasions, you get credited with a million dollars. But it takes a lot of time (or if you like, fills in a lot of insomnia) to get that far. In my one attempt I finished 107th when my aces up were beaten by a straight. I found the game both monotonous, because it's so repetitive, and quite interesting to play, because of the high degree of concentration required. One comment by a player on screen I liked: "Think long, think wrong!"

A computer game called Hoyle Poker offered more sense of personalities – though they did not seem to play according to their names – for instance the Irish widow Mrs. O'Shea, a clipped-voice Britisher and a Western dude. Instead, a series of mildly amusing comments issued from these types, as the betting went around – the Britisher:

"I'll wager my villa in France, I'm going to give you a kick in the pants", or Elayne, a blonde bimbo: "Goody, goody, I win all the money." Or Mrs. O'Shea, "I'm not a call girl, I'm a call granny." By the time you've heard "I'll bet my condo in Colorado I'm going to kick your Aspen," two or three times, the novelty has faded. Hoyle Poker has the advantage that the player can choose between Hold 'em, Omaha, Omaha high-low, seven card stud, five card draw and five card draw lowball, and that you can vary the stakes.

"Real live players are much more diverse than any computer poker program," warns one expert.[3] "If you play against one program long enough, you start to be able to predict exactly how your opponents will react in various situations. Your ability to read your opponents becomes almost uncanny. Unfortunately, while some live players are predictable, many are not . . . The best advice for using computer poker programs may be to just not play them too much."

The bottom line of current legislative manoeuvres in the United States is a concerted attempt by the states to establish their jurisdiction over gambling in the home. It is equally clear that law enforcement agencies are reluctant to devote scarce resources to policing a murky area. A comprehensive analysis of the whole sector[4] concluded that the US Justice Department recognises that as a practical matter there is nothing it can do about people who operate gambling businesses

[3] 'The dangers of Poker Software' by Johann Ruegg, *The Intelligent Gambler*, November, 1995

[4] *The United States Gross Annual Wager* by Eugene Martin Christiansen, published by International Gaming and Wagering Business, August 1997

outside of the United States. According to the author of the report, Eugene Christiansen, a leading gaming analyst in the US, some 'near-certainties' about gambling in the home could be predicted.

One is that major telecommunications companies would not participate and large amounts of capital would not be invested in interactive gambling businesses unless those businesses were endorsed by government.

Another certainty is the existence of substantial latent demand for in-home gambling services. "The thousand-odd mostly rudimentary Internet gambling sites out there in cyberspace are ample evidence of the public's appetite for these services." So long as the combination of certain demand and uncertain legality persists, Christiansen suggested, the in-home gambling market would continue to be supplied by 'kitchen table' Internet entrepreneurs.

The future of gambling in the home might resemble sports betting in most of North America today, Christiansen concluded: "illegal, unregulated, ubiquitous, and the special preserve of entrepreneurial operators able to tolerate the business environment of supplying a grey market."

It is easy enough to get started. Advertisements for online casinos proliferate. For instance, full-page ads in a magazine called *Chance* (March-April issue 1999, published in New York) proffered Golden Palace 'Suit Yourself . . . with 28 casino games to choose from'; Intercasino – 'Baby needs a new pair of shoes . . . Experience the thrill of live casino wagering at home'; Goldmine Internet casino – 'Call now for your free welcome kit, free credits, special gift and much, much more'.

Other ads stress the casino operation's honesty, for instance Lloyds 'The Safest Place to Bet – Licensed in Antigua, 8 yrs. experience, Payouts any day of the week, Activate your account in five minutes, All plays recorded and computerized, Private and confidential' (*DoubleDown*, January 1999, published in Chicago).

An article in the magazine *DoubleDown* entitled 'Beating the House Without Leaving it' noted: "For some gamblers, the lights, sounds, climate and patrons – not to mention a lengthy wait for a table – all serve as a distraction from the main reason to travel to a casino to begin with – the gambling. Conversely, casual gamblers and first-timers are often intimidated and overwhelmed by the general casino experience. Gambling on the Internet has allowed all of these people a very attractive alternative." Primarily, convenience.

Another advertisement offered Internet gaming software (*Casino Player*, February 1999, published in Las Vegas). "MicroGaming Systems is the world's largest supplier of online Internet casino software. We were the first company in the world to offer real money Internet gaming . . . MicroGaming is well aware that the biggest concern raised by online casino players is that of whether the games they are playing are rigged or biased in any way."

To counter this, MicroGaming claimed its systems had been designed by experts, tested by third parties and that its expected payback percentages met or (in most cases) exceeded standard Nevada pay-outs.

"We believe that increased public awareness of the issues of fairness and integrity of online casinos can only benefit the industry and players alike by leading to the weeding out of any fly-by-night operators."

You mean lurking in the dark corners of this cybernet realm of super-honesty there are some bad guys? Well, I never!

No one is really sure how the Internet will develop over the next five to ten years. In 1997 it was estimated that $7 to $8 billion in goods and services was traded over the Internet. The popularity of the gaming sector reflects this growth. One estimate was $600m. wagered in 1999. Nelson Rose cited guestimates of $10 billion a year in revenue for online gaming by the end of the century, which would require $100 billion being wagered. Current volume, he suggested, appears to be in the range of less than $2 billion. Internet gaming in the US – relative to overall gambling – is relatively small, he opined, and likely to stay that way for the next few years.

Still, the frenzied enthusiasm of the public for Internet stocks on Wall Street, which occurred at the end of 1998, showed how widespread and intense the craze for gambling in this sector is. All the stocks which rose so fast, sometimes doubling or trebling in a few hours, rebounded down again – as they always do in speculative bubbles. "Internet gaming popped up because of the Wild West approach of the Internet. If someone can view pornography on the Internet, and if they can also trade stocks, why can't they gamble?" inquired, very reasonably, an article in *Casino Player*.

As a commercial activity, Internet gambling has the potential for large rewards for the operators. This process is a cause of concern, according to one psychologist who has studied 'technological addictions'.

Such addictions are described by Dr. Mark Griffiths as non-chemical (behavioural) addictions, which involve human-machine interaction. They can either be passive (like television) or active (as in computer games) and usually contain inducing and reinforcing features.

Under the heading 'technological addictions' could be included hacking and Internet usage, video and computer games, fruit machines and pinball, and virtual reality. It is of course the business of people like Griffiths, who is a lecturer in psychology at the University of Plymouth, to find 'problems' in these activities. While admitting that there is little evidence for technological addictions as a distinct clinical entity, Griffiths takes the view that the effects of excess are very similar to the effects of familiar addictions like alcohol, drugs and gambling.

The Internet, in short, could easily be the focus of obsessive or compulsive behaviour like gambling. "These new technologies may provide many people with their first exposure to the world of gambling and could be argued to be more enticing than previous non-technological incarnations."[5]

How far will it go? A revealing comparison can be made between gambling and the movies[6]. Just as the movie industry has moved from the distribution of commercial movies from city centre theatres to suburban shopping malls and on to the home in the form of video tapes, pay-per-view and cable channels, so

[5] *Internet Gambling: A Cause for Concern?* by Dr. Mark Griffiths, GamCare News, 1997

[6] *The Economics of Casino Gambling* by William R Eadington, Journal of Economic Perspectives, 1999.

the evolution of casino-style gambling is moving from destination resorts to suburban casinos, and then on to various gaming opportunities in the home or the neighbourhood.

A paragraph in *The Times* in London caught my attention. "Are you worried about how much time you, or someone you know, spends on the Internet whether at work or at home?" it asked. If so, it advised, visit *www.netaddiction.com*. "It sounds like a joke, but there are people for whom Internet addiction is a real problem and the site has lots of advice for them."

The Center for On-Line Addiction billed itself as the world's first consultation firm and virtual clinic for cyber-related addiction. What is Internet addiction? It listed five specific types. 1. Cybersexual addiction (addictions to adult chat rooms or cyberporn). 2. Cyber-relationship addiction (online friendships made in chat room newsgroups that replace real life friends and family). 3. Net compulsions (compulsive online gambling, auction addiction and online trading). 4. Information overload (compulsive web surfing or database searches). 5. Computer addiction (obsessive computer game playing).

How can you tell if you are addicted? Some typical warning signs were listed, such as: Do you feel preoccupied with the Internet, do you feel the need to use the Internet for increasing amounts of time, and have you repeatedly made unsuccessful efforts to control, cut back or stop Internet use?

My own problem with the Internet was different from all of these. It was a serious distortion of my phone bill! Local calls in Britain, unlike America, are not free. When my first bill after going on the net came through from the telephone company, my bank refused to pay it. Anyway, those people who answered 'Yes' to these sorts of questions were advised to read a book called *Caught in the Net* by Dr. Kimberly S. Young, which offered a winning strategy for recovery. With translations in German, Italian, Danish and Japanese, the sales pitch added.

To return to the more scholarly approach of Dr. Mark Griffiths – what makes the Internet addictive to some people? For many people the very idea that a person can become addicted (should one better say 'hooked'?) is intuitively nonsense, Griffiths adds, because their concept of addiction usually involves the ingestion of a drug. But there are several non-drug forms of behaviour which can be regarded as potentially addictive – gambling, overeating and overslimming, sex, exercise and computer game playing.

People perform different types of activity on the net, for example mailing, information browsing, file transferring, socialising, role-game playing and so on. But how can one define the object of the addiction, Griffiths asks.

The process of typing, the medium of communication, aspects of its style (such as the lack of face-to-face interaction), the information that can be obtained (like pornography), the playing of fantasy-role games and talking to others in chat rooms are all potentially addictive traits of Internet use.

The structural characteristics of the machine are also very important. Such features, which are common to slot machines, include the speed of the action, light and colour effects, sound effects, graphics and skill or pseudo-skill buttons which enhance the activity.

As Professor Rose pointed out, the trouble (in making provision for legal controls) lies in deciding whether the Internet is like direct mail or like television. Although the Internet is interactive, like mail or telephone, websites, he says, are passive and the user has to receive the message, like television or radio. The net seems to have characteristics of both mail and TV. And there is no stopping it at the border.

With the opening of Bellagio, Steve Wynn claimed that "people who normally would go to hotels in Paris will come to Las Vegas".

What an intriguing claim! Leaving aside the point that Bellagio is in fact named after an Italian resort, and not the French capital, Wynn was suggesting that the excellence of his new hotel was such that there would be no need to go to Paris – where, his implication was, the best hotels had been located up to now. "We wanted to build a hotel so pre-emptive, so much better than any in the world, that people who never came to Nevada would go see it."

All right – a bit of boasting on the occasion of a licensing hearing is to be expected and quite acceptable. Bellagio, which opened on October 15, 1998, cost $1.6 billion. A night in one of its suites may well be top-notch – but the experience is so different it can't really be compared with a night at, say, the Ritz in Paris.

Still, Wynn touched on a point about appearance and reality which in a sense exemplifies the appeal of Las Vegas in the age of cyberspace. All the replicas of famous sites and locations in Vegas – do they in a sense spare the traveller the trouble of booking a ticket and making the journey to see the originals?

In Las Vegas, we have on offer a Roman forum, an Egyptian pyramid, New York's skyline, Arthurian romance, a Polynesian rainforest, properties inspired by Venice, Monte Carlo, Paris, a wax museum of the stars, and so on. Mock heroic or tongue-in-cheek as they may be, they give the visitor, in a sort of back-to-front way (seeing the copy before the reality) an impression of 'the real thing'.

In Europe when people want to be amused, says Umberto Eco, the celebrated semiotician[7], they go to a 'house' of amusement (whether a cinema, theatre or casino); sometimes a 'park' is created, which may seem a 'city', but only metaphorically.

"In the United States, on the contrary, as everyone knows, there exist amusement cities. Las Vegas is one example; it is focused on gambling and entertainment, its architecture is totally artificial . . . a completely new phenomenon in city planning, a 'message' city, entirely made up of signs, not a city like the others, which communicate in order to function, but rather a city that functions in order to communicate." (Though Las Vegas, as he admits, has now become a 'real' city, of a million people.)

Americans can now get an impression of a whole range of famous historical sites – for casinos will certainly go on inventing them – which give some sort of 'take' on the original. Never mind that the result is usually not just fake, but comically inappropriate, kitsch to a degree.

According to Professor Eco, "there is a constant in the average American imagination and taste, for which the past

[7] *Travels in Hyperreality*, 1986

must be preserved and celebrated in full-scale authentic copy." He cites President Lyndon Johnson's mausoleum in Austin, Texas, with its full-scale model of the Oval Office. A 'completely real' fake, which connotes, he says, an America of hyperreality.

People have stock images of the Pyramids or Ancient Rome, acquired from school or TV or the movies, and these places in Vegas, though designed first and last to *sell* to the customer, offer an amusing approximation. "This isn't like ancient Egypt," a guide confided to me at Luxor, "but to our visitors, it *is*." Europeans who may have had the good fortune to visit the real forum or the real pyramids, thanks to living on the other side of the world, should not feel superior. We all share in this experience. The statue of Michelangelo's David as presented by Caesars Palace is larger than the original – more for your money!

Aren't these signs and wonders in Las Vegas like the images of cyberspace? The difference being that they are represented in physical or architectural form. The whole resort is 'fake', offering imitations of reality which in their variety and energy elevate the place into a new 'reality' of its own. In other words a vacation trip round the sights of Las Vegas bears some resemblance to surfing the net.

At Bellagio, Steve Wynn made the most audacious move yet seen, to go beyond the fake and the pretend by opening an art gallery showing Impressionist and other classic paintings – 'the real thing' indeed. What a concept! Who had ever imagined seeing art, original paintings, in the middle of the desert? Not copies, like replicas of *The Last Supper* which are a dime a dozen at tourist sites; or electronic images of Leonardo's work, which you can study on the net in close-up.

In sum, appearance and reality have become so interwoven one can hardly separate one from the other. The point about gambling on the net is that it can work, in parallel, but in a different way, from real gambling. Each has its place, like paintings and copies of paintings.

6

Playing with Words

Forgive me . . . but I know that you're still rather frivolous and may be capable of gambling . . .
Actually I haven't got any money . . . in order to lose it one first has to have it.
The Gambler, Fyodor Dostoyevsky

Of all the hundreds and thousands of book on gambling or about gambling, is there any one book which stands out? I suppose Dostoyevsky's long short story *The Gambler* would be top of most people's list. His account of the gambling experience is so vivid – in the sense of being vigorous and lifelike – that you never forget it. Each time you read it, you feel again the author's passion for gambling that lay behind the story, and gave it its intensity. Dostoyevsky wrote it fast to get money to pay off his gambling debts.

"His young wife Anna Grigorevna was not spared the misery of having to pawn clothes and other possessions to enable him to recoup his losses. The obsession was intermittent. Sometimes Dostoyevsky resisted the temptation, but Anna Grigorevna's diaries and reminiscences, no less than Dostoyevsky's own correspondence, tell the awful tale of debt, pawnbrokers, outpourings of guilt and begging letters and pleas to friends."[1]

Dostoyevsky had a system. "I watched those players attentively for four days . . . Please don't think that I'm bragging about the fact that I didn't lose in saying that I know the secret of not losing, but winning. I really do know the secret. It's very stupid and simple and amounts to ceaseless self-control at all stages of the game and not getting excited. That's all there is to it. That way you can't lose—"

Up to this point we are all in admiring agreement with Fyodor and his insight into gambling, but then he adds the fatal misperception – "and are bound to win." (Letter of 20 August 1863, from Paris, recounting his experience in Wiesbaden.)

He goes on, showing rare self-awareness: "But that's not the point. The point is whether, once you know the secret, you are capable of exploiting it."

Three weeks later, the author was writing to his brother from Turin: "You write to ask how I could possibly lose everything while travelling with someone I love . . ." His system, he explained, worked wonderfully, to start with, ". . . how could I not get carried away and believe that if I followed my system strictly I should be sure to win? And I needed money, for myself, for you, for my wife, for writing my novel . . ." He did win, at first, and this whetted his appetite. But then: "Suddenly I started to lose,

[1]Introduction by Malcolm Jones to the World's Classics edition

couldn't control myself and lost everything . . . In Geneva I pawned my watch."

Well, we've all been there, done that. The difference is that Dostoyevsky was a genius. His name is like a beacon which casts its light forward over all the writers, in the century after him, who have gambled and lost and emulated him in trying to recreate the experience and make sense of it.

It would be too much to list them all. My aim here is to narrow the field by looking at how writers have reacted to the most influential place in gambling in the modern world, Las Vegas. I cite Dostoyevsky, not just because he is a major figure in gambling fiction but because Las Vegas brings out the downside in writers, their sense of despair. The whole place, with its brighter-than-bright exterior concealing a darker-than-dark abyss, offers a perfect 'objective correlative' for personal depression and artistic gloom. If you are feeling lousy, if your marriage is breaking up, what better town than Las Vegas to ponder the transience of this sad world?

Naturally there are exceptions, the most notable example being the man in the white suit. The sheer energy of Tom Wolfe's adverse judgement on Las Vegas carries such an exciting charge that he wins you over completely. His piece entitled *Las Vegas (What?) Las Vegas (Can't Hear You! Too Noisy) Las Vegas!!!* (1963) is a classic. It begins, you may recall, with the word "hernia" being repeated over and over and over again. "Hernia, hernia, hernia, HERNia, Hernia . . ." for a whole paragraph.

Raymond is standing at the craps table, zonked out of his mind after two and a half days without sleep, and this is the only noise he can hear at that point. *Hernia, hernia, hernia, HERNia, Hernia* . . . Wolfe is right, it is the characteristic background blur at the craps table, in the middle of the casino floor, when you are that far gone. The security guards ease Raymond out before he gets into trouble. But Wolfe has much else to celebrate about Las Vegas, notably the signs, their shapes and colours, the fizz of it all.

For the grand début at Monte Carlo as a resort in 1879 (only a few years after Dostoyevsky's fateful visit to 'Roulettenberg') the architect Charles Garnier designed an opera house for the Place du Casino, and Sarah Bernhardt read a symbolic poem. As Wolfe pointed out, "For the début of Las Vegas as a resort in 1946, Bugsy Siegel hired Abbott and Costello, and there, in a way, you have it all." (The headliner in fact was Jimmy Durante.) Wolfe might have added that the immortal Sarah Bernhardt was wont to gamble away her fees at the gaming tables, which shows that the Monégasque management was not altogether blinded by culture.

No one can match Wolfe when it comes to dissecting the funny side of social mores, but the weirdest, most frenetic account of Las Vegas is Hunter S. Thompson's celebrated spree *Fear and Loathing in Las Vegas* (1971), reprinted I don't know how many times. This is the gambling city as seen through the dilated eyes of a guy stoned out of his skull on a cornucopia of drugs – grass, mescaline, acid, cocaine, uppers, downers, screamers, laughers, raw ether, amyls, plus quantities of tequila, rum and beer. This is what Thompson and friend packed into the trunk of their car when he set off for a life-defying rampage through casino culture.

"Every now and then when your life gets complicated

and the weasels start closing in, the only real cure is to load up on heinous chemicals and then drive like a bastard from Hollywood to Las Vegas." Ostensibly, Thompson was on a magazine assignment, looking for the American Dream. His quest turns into a series of drugged-up encounters with casino staff, police officers, bartenders and waitresses, which end in farce, shocks, threats and hasty exits, and the rapid ingestion of more and more stimulants.

In the brief intervals of this hallucinogenic progress, like the momentary pattern of colours caught when you shake up a kaleidoscope, surreal glimpses of Las Vegas flash by. The Flamingo hotel like a huge under-financed Playboy Club in the middle of the desert . . . Circus-Circus like the Sixth Reich . . . "This is what the whole hep world would be doing on Saturday night if the Nazis had won the war".

> *The ground floor is full of gaming tables, like all the other casinos . . . but the place is about four stories high, in the style of a circus tent, and all manner of strange County-Fair/Polish Carnival madness is going on up in this space. Right above the gambling tables the Forty Flying Carazito Brothers are doing a high-wire trapeze act, along with four muzzled Wolverines and the Six Nymphet Sisters from San Diego . . . so you're down on the main floor playing blackjack and the stakes are getting high when suddenly you chance to look up, and there, right smack above your head is a half-naked fourteen-year old girl being chased through the air by a snarling wolverine, which is suddenly locked in a death battle with two silver-painted Polacks who come swinging down from opposite balconies and meet in mid-air on the wolverine's neck . . .*

Las Vegas is not a good town for psychedelic drugs, Thompson concludes. Reality itself is too twisted.

And what about the gambling? That does not interest the author at all, which is hardly surprising given his condition. Eventually, Thompson and his attorney, a huge Samoan no less crazed and drugged than he is, drive out to a place they are told might be 'the American Dream'. It used to be known as the old Psychiatrist's Club, on Paradise. The only people who hang out there, recalls a guy at a fast food stand, who gives them directions, are "a bunch of pushers, peddlers, uppers and downers, all that stuff". Sounds all right!

Is it a night-time place or all day? they inquire. It never stops. Hunter gets out there to find a huge slab of cracked, scorched concrete in a vacant lot full of tall weeds. The owner of a gas station across the road says the place had burned down about three years ago. A little bit of this town, Hunter concludes, goes a very long way. A funny book indeed, which says a lot more about the author (who can sometimes act very nasty) than Las Vegas.

When it comes to expressing depression about Las Vegas, two writers share the *palme noire*, Joan Didion and John Gregory Dunne. Didion's *Play It As It Lays* was published in 1970. Dunne's *Vegas – A Memoir of a Dark Season* came out in 1974. Though not exactly a husband-and-wife team, the fact that the authors were (and are) married adds a certain piquancy to their very different narratives.

Play It As It Lays (which Joan Didion dedicated to John) is the story of a young woman drifting in the milieu of spoiled, beautiful movie people, whose lives criss-cross Los Angeles and Las Vegas, a backdrop in emotional terms as arid as the Mojave desert. Maria, the heroine, is going through a mental breakdown. The experience is seen mainly through her deepening unhappiness, at losing a child, at failing to connect with her husband, lover, friends, her own future.

In her desolation, the evocation of a particular side of Las Vegas' smart-life, rich, empty, corrupt, depicted from the inside, is horribly convincing. Take this chilling paragraph for example, which distils Maria's feeling, or her lack of feeling, about her life.

> *Maria made a list of the things she would never do. She would never: walk through the Sands or Caesars alone after midnight. She would never: bawl at a party, do S & M unless she wanted to, borrow furs from Abe Lipsey, deal. She would never: carry a Yorkshire in Beverly Hills.*

Play It As It Lays takes its title from the advice Maria's father gave her as a child – life is a crap game. It goes as it lays, don't do it the hard way. She was, she says, raised to believe that what came in on the next roll would always be better than what went out on the last.

Maria finds that this easy gambler's optimism, which only half carried the family through even in the old days, when they lived out in the desert – now a nuclear testing ground – no longer applies. It is hopelessly out of synch with her adult life. She has nowhere to turn, caught up in the artificial existence of selfish, self-indulgent people, playing around with drugs and movie-making. In the vacuum of her life, she drives endlessly up and down the Los Angeles freeways.

What game was it supposed to be that she is playing? Nothing counts. All warmth and sympathy have gone. Her disillusionment is not a story about Las Vegas, but it conveys more intensely than any other novel the desolation of Las Vegas – *hernia, hernia* – when life goes wrong.

By contrast, John Gregory Dunne fled to Las Vegas to get away from himself and work through a bad patch in his marriage. The result was his *A Memoir of a Dark Season.* It is a look at Las Vegas from the bottom of the pile. Three characters, a hooker, a comedian and a private detective, expose their desperate search for the grail of success – big bucks in one way or another – and reveal at the same time a lot about Las Vegas low life.

And low it is. Gambling hardly gets a look in: the universal hustle is for cheap sex, preferably free sex. The hooker dispenses it, in the intervals between getting busted for soliciting, the failed comedian talks about it, with less and less conviction, the detective tracks down spouses who have offended sexually against each other.

Dunne saw a sign, emblazoned in gold letters on a roulette wheel, on a billboard in Hollywood: VISIT LAS VEGAS BEFORE YOUR NUMBER'S UP. The message had a Delphic fascination for him. It persuaded him to make the trip and immerse himself in the people he met there, their seedy true-life confessions. (He was the kind of stranger people would immediately confide in.) Las Vegas offered salvation without commitment, a way of easing his own nervous breakdown by peeping, like a voyeur, into the even more desolate lives of these denizens of the 'too much fun' club.

Dunne strikes up quick friendships with all manner of people (the exact opposite of the fictional Maria of *Play It As It Lays*) from the very start of his stay. "If you gamble, sir, good luck," says the ageing bellhop who shows him to his room, "and if you need a little company, you just give me a ring, hear?" Each of the trio of central characters he befriends uncovers more and more of the dark side of Vegas.

> The hooker: *She had been cruising since midnight with no luck. The secret of cruising was to keep moving. Caesars first, then the Tropicana, then the Sands. No luck. No more than two drinks in any casino. Stay for more than two drinks without making a connection and hotel security begins to get nervous. The hotel draws a fine line. They like the girls available for the roller who wants a pop, but then they don't want the casino to look like a lamppost.*

As the second main character, the private detective says, reassuringly: "Everyone in Vegas knows what everyone else is doing – so what?" Or the warm-up comedian, who comes ahead of the star-name of the dinner show, a showbiz entertainer, the performer whom the audience has paid good money to see: "The warm-up comic has forty-five minutes and functions basically as a high colonic, getting the audience through dinner, one trip to the john, a little juice on board, loosening them up for the headliner. He stands there, a guy with six tuxedos in his closet, every one with the sky-blue lining . . . launches a fusillade of one-liners . . . back and forth across the stage."

Yet a sort of gritty optimism keeps breaking through as these Las Vegas characters struggle to make a living. Somehow, the therapy of empathising with their futile lives works for the author of *A Memoir of a Dark Season*. After 200 pages he is calling his wife on the phone. Soon after that he is on his way back.

A sunny optimism is what lifts the heroine of *The*

Desert Rose by Larry McMurtry (1983). She is a showgirl, once loved and cherished as the most beautiful of all the showgirls, but now, at almost 39, on her way out of the show. McMurtry's novel (written in only three weeks) is perhaps the best book about ordinary day-to-day life in Las Vegas.

It shows people as they are, working, rushing their coffee breaks between shows, trying to get their cars fixed and do their household chores, having fast friendships like fast food, the daily round set against the non-stop glitz of the Strip casinos, which are not, for these people, places of entertainment but places of work.

Harmony, the showgirl, has an even more attractive daughter, named Pepper (the names say a lot about the characters). Pepper, at the age of 16, is being groomed for the role of lead dancer in the 'tits and feathers' show in which her mother has displayed her charms (suspended on a disc above the stage) all her showgirl life. It's a tough trade for Harmony, to be told she has to quit the show, sacked, to enable her daughter to take over as star. The producer tells her frankly, a mother and daughter on the same stage could lead to some tricky publicity.

But Harmony can take it. She is none too strong at standing up for herself, but she has a special quality, "the ability to see the bright side". It takes courage to do that, a friend tells her. She is a person who likes to think about the good things that could happen rather than the bad kinds of things. And one of the good things about Las Vegas was that it enabled her to become a showgirl, a feathered beauty, whereas anywhere else, she feels, nobody would have known what to do with her.

Harmony's optimism sort of wins through ("sort of" is how the characters express their thoughts and feelings in this story). Actually, the author is sort of in love with Harmony: one of the nicest things that can happen, McMurtry says in a preface to the paperback, is to have your characters teach you something, that optimism is a form of courage, for example. That is Harmony's theme, and through her it gives Las Vegas a warm glow – even if, overall, the book is smudged by sentimentality.

Which – a sentimental glow – is more than can be said for the Las Vegas of Mario Puzo's novel *Fools Die* (1978). Most of the action happens in a big casino in the heart of the Strip called the Hotel Xanadu. The slick picture it gives of sex and corruption has, I presume, coloured the imagination of tens of thousands of readers around the world as to what life in a top casino is like. Everybody in management is cheating on each other, from the president on down, so in the end no one knows who is hustling whom: cheap and sleazy sex is on demand (at $100 a shot) from every female employee on the casino staff: overall, the characters act out their lives with the same deadening amorality which was the pervasive principle (or lack of principle) of Puzo's *The Godfather* (1970).

Fools Die presents a very one-sided view of Vegas as a resort but amid all the narrative schlock it does convey a clear perception of what gamblers and gambling are about. Mario Puzo, as he admits, has played for high stakes himself. (In his photo essay *Inside Las Vegas* Puzo says he believes that gambling has bettered his character, kept him out of prison and helped him raise his family.) The opening scenes in the casino offer some sharp observations about gambling – a house shill, indifferent to winning or losing, is described as "boringly immortal", the faint roar from the action on the casino floor is heard high up in a hotel room like surf on a distant beach; or the curious aloneness and togetherness of gambling – "He loved the feeling of being solitary in the crowd of people and the gambling hum. To be alone without being lonely. To be friends with strangers for an hour and never see them again."

And the guiding principle of the casino, the golden rule which management lives by: *percentages*. "Percentages never lie. We built all these hotels on percentages. We stay rich on the percentage." As the hero of the story is advised by the casino president: "You can lose faith in everything, religion and God, women and love, good and evil, war and peace. You name it. But the percentage will always stand fast." (Did Dostoyevsky understand this? Probably in his lucid moments, but – like the rest of us – not when in the grip of his obsession.)

Beating the percentage, as all gamblers hope and pray to do in the short run, has its disadvantage, too. The *leitmotif* of *Fools Die* is the gambler who beats the house, wins a fortune, and somehow or other can't live with his success. In this story, nobody comes out winning. Even the hero, who at least manages to stay alive, concludes: "I knew now the single fact that no matter how carefully I planned, no matter how cunning I was, lies or good deeds done, I couldn't really 'win'."

The story of high life and corruption in *Fools Die* is a long way from the workaday cares of the people who serve the customers in *The Desert Rose* but Puzo knows the high roller milieu from the inside; he is revealing about foreign gamblers, particularly the Japanese.

> *The English were immediately written off despite their history of being the biggest losers of the nineteenth century.*[2] *The end of the British Empire had meant the end of their high rollers . . . the French were also written off. The French didn't travel and would never stand for the extra house double zero on the Vegas wheel . . . But the Germans and Italians were wooed . . . there was something in the high flying Vegas style that appealed to the Teutonic spirit . . . The Mexican and South American gamblers were even bigger prizes . . .*

The Japanese in the story all wear black business suits, badly tailored by western standards, with white shirts and black ties. The party arriving at the airport looked like a band of very earnest clerks instead of the ruling board of Japan's richest and most powerful business conglomerate:

> *. . . the band of ten Japanese terrorized the casinos of Vegas. They would travel together and gamble together at the same baccarat table. When Fummiro [the leader] had the shoe, they all bet the limit with him on the bank . . . they played with a joie de vivre more Italian than Oriental. Fummiro would whip the sides of the shoe and bang on the table when he dealt himself a natural eight or nine. He was a passionate gambler and gloated over winning a two-thousand dollar bet . . . the band of ten men in their shiny black suits . . . were a frightening sight, marching ten strong into a casino, looking*

[2]Mario Puzo has his own way with history.

like undertakers come to collect the corpse of the casino's bankroll.

But of course the percentage gets them too. The happy gambler is the man who just plays for the helluvit, for fun, like the narrator in *Fools Die*. "I made five-dollar bets and bet all the numbers. I won and I lost. I drifted into my old gambling patterns, moving from craps to blackjack and roulette. Soft, easy, dreamy gambling, betting small, winning and losing, playing loose percentages . . . gambling was fun, that was all." Let's give Mario Puzo credit. These are wise words.

Although it's not about Las Vegas, a book I liked a lot is *Bob the Gambler*. This short novel by Frederick Barthelme (1997) reflects the Vegas experience at one remove, in Mississippi. It is the story of an easy-going, American family consisting of mother, teenage daughter and stepfather, who are all very fond of each other but somehow slightly dysfunctional. Bob and Jewel, his wife, fall into gambling at the local casino, but instead of being hapless, helpless victims, they more or less deliberately set about ruining themselves, by going in too far.

Barthelme's style has been likened by one critic to a kind of literary pop art. In *Bob the Gambler* he uses simple, clear, familiar images drawn from everyday life (like a Warhol painting) in the trailer-park belt of Biloxi, and melds them into a collage of modern American life, at once simple and evocative. Here are the opening lines to illustrate the point:

What I'd always liked about Biloxi was the decay, the things falling apart, the crap along the beach, the skeletons of abandoned hotels, the trashy warehouses and the rundown piers jutting out into the dirty water, so I wasn't thrilled that in the last five years our dinky coast town had been turned into an outlet-mall version of Las Vegas with a dozen cartoon casinos, lots of gussied-up Motel 6 hotel rooms, an ocean of slicked-back hair, and a big increase in unsavoury tourists.

It turns out that 'Bob the Gambler' is an ironic nickname which he acquires from Jewel's enthusiasm to try, at long last, the local casino. The gambling scenes are extremely well done but not at all what you might expect. This is the interior life of the downmarket local casino, the sort which has spread right across the United States, which is, in a way, almost a social club. The staff and the slots players all know each other and the dealers actually want their neighbours to win, if they can. Naturally Jewel starts out winning, but in a casual, off-hand style of play, and naturally they go on to blow most of their money – but in a Hey! look-at-us-acting-like-morons way.

On the night of utter disaster, the shift manager, ever so gently, tries to dissuade Bob from destroying himself.

"How're things?" he said.

"Don't know yet," I said. "Got any advice?"

"Go home?" Phil said.

"Who you got dealing there?" I said.

Phil Post was always pleasant, always commiserating, urging us to leave when we were ahead or even when we got even after a bad run of cards . . .

"Nobody's dealing there, that's the point," he said. "I'm trying to save you some money."

"I might win, though," I said.

"I might date Marilyn Monroe in the afterlife," Phil said. "But I'm not making a book on it."

The story is not really about gambling. It turns out that *Bob the Gambler* is a celebration of family life, in which Bob and his zingy 14-year-old stepdaughter form a funny, affectionate bond. He also works out a new deal to take care of his mother (or is it the other way round?) who is living a banal sitcom existence apart from his Dad. The gambling is central: but in the underlying pull of the novel less important as an entity in itself, than as the spark which rekindles their life and brings them together as a family.

Bob and Jewel are uncomplaining, resigned, almost happy at losing out. Their acceptance of their low rent existence is ironic and self-aware. Rather than grand despair at the vast meaningless of life, Barthelme's vision of gambling is like Dostoyevsky on Prozac.

And then, some months later, I came across the 'real life' experience which inspired this gambling novel. It was related in a long 'personal history' by Frederick Barthelme and his brother Steven, entitled *Good Losers* published in *The New Yorker* (March 8, 1999).[3] The magazine billed the co-authors as teaching fiction writing at the University of Southern Mississippi. The article described their gambling spree. It all began, as it usually does, with a lucky win. It ended in disaster.

Yes, it can happen to university professors, just like the rest of us! But this was not the usual disaster. Rick and

[3]Later pubished as a book titled *Double Down – Reflections on Gambling and Loss*

Steve, in this story, are into all-night blackjack sessions on 'the boats' of the Mississippi coast casinos.

"The walk from the garage to the casino is all nerves – like the walk from the locker room to football field. They swagger, they lope. It's jokes and jitters. They imagine stacks of chips. Everything is still possible." Maybe it's the air-conditioning, but as soon as they open the doors, they're gone, ". . . they're washed with treated air, the din, the scent of money, liquor, smoke. Adrenaline and aftershave. They're keyed up now, giddy, hopeful. They walk with a sure step. Something is suddenly clear, precise, desired."

What differentiates this pair (literary fellows, after all) is that they *know* what they are doing as they lose their bundles and deplete their savings. So why do they do it? At first it was entertainment. They would go in, wander, play the slot machines, play video poker, tell jokes, come home. After their mother died – both parents had an influential role in their lives – they no longer played little slots. They played higher stakes games. Dealers stopped to say hello and cashiers knew them by name.

"There was a new intensity to our play, so subtle that we only vaguely noted it, putting it down to a combination of factors – a feeling that we ought to be able to figure out a way to win, coupled with the knowledge (from books we'd been reading) that we probably weren't going to win and, added to that, the recognition that our gambling wasn't 'sensible'."

A year later their father died. He left them a substantial legacy. They went on losing, at first not so much, but then a lot. And then a lot more. They felt somehow "it wasn't really our money, it was his." They ran through their inheritance, a combined loss of some quarter of a million dollars. "At the table, losing our money, we were all smiles, as if it were nothing. In fact, it felt like nothing. Money isn't money in a casino."

There was also a dark side. They write of "a unique despair", gambling in the recognition that you have no chance, that you will lose whatever you do. How do you know? "That is also a puzzle. You begin to sense that for all the mathematics, the calculations, the odds, the multiplying strategies of working the percentages, some wholly other thing is at work, some loopy otherworldly thing. It seems built into the cards." In contrast, when you win, like hitting a jackpot, it is an experience of perfection.

The money was not the point. The win, when everything all comes together, is practically a mystical experience:

> *The perfect thing had happened. The possibility of perfection was something most of our friends and colleagues in the university where we worked no longer believed in . . . But everybody in the casino believed. However crude, however dizzy, however self-deluded these people may have been, they knew how to hope, how to imagine life as something other than a dreary chore. They imagined that something wonderful might happen, something that could change their lives. This was their fool's secret, one they shared with drunks, artists, and children, all of whom they resembled.*

They found that they understood the gamblers in the casino better (and perhaps liked them more) than the men and women in the university where they worked.

The brothers knew what to expect – they were supposed

to get so intoxicated with their vice that they lost everything, in total ruin but their story has an ending which would have puzzled, not just Dostoyevsky, but pretty well everyone. After playing blackjack all night, several security people came up to the table, escorted them out and accused them of cheating – even though they had lost nearly $10,000 that night. Later, they were indicted and charged with committing a felony.

The *New Yorker* article ended by noting that if they were found guilty, they would face a fine and two years in prison. The book recounts a spirited defence to these absurd charges, which were finally dropped.

Many writers have tried to capture Las Vegas in its different moods and aspects – sleaze and depression on one side, glamour and excitement on the other. But no one has yet captured Las Vegas with the imaginative truth of art, in the way that Mark Twain caught the Mississippi and made it his own, or in our own time writers have celebrated favourite places like London, Dublin, Paris, New England.

David Kranes (a writer who teaches at the University of Utah) to my mind comes closest to it. He has caught the nihilistic, floating, surreal quality of living in Las Vegas, of a life strangely removed and heightened from everyday living, better than anyone else. In his short stories, the identity of the characters seems to shift in their uncertainty about themselves, and what they are doing, in ways which evoke the essential experience of Las Vegas. Here is the opening paragraph of his story called *Who I am is*:

> *You're staying at the MGM Grand and it's between late May and early September and you're by the pool on your*

> *chaise with something that's got gin or vodka or sherbet in it and the page girl over the p.a. keeps saying: 'Mr. Leland Hetchgar: telephone, please! Mr. Leland Hetchgar.' And then again, five minutes later: 'Mr. Leland Hetchgar: long distance!' Every five minutes or so, it repeats. You're there. And I'm being paged: 'Mr. Leland Hetchgar!' And you're wondering who the hell I am. Well, that's who. That's me. I'm him. I'm the guy who does business by the pool five months at least a year. I'm Lee Hetchgar.*

This story can't be summed up by its plot because there is no plot – nothing happens – the central character drifts around town, taking calls, having a manicure, taking a girl to dinner, teaching her to play dice – but all in a kind of suspended state, as if watching himself and listening to himself, but without getting answers. At one point he goes to a party for a meeting of magazine distributors.

> *'Sally Ann, sweetheart. I've never read a paperback book.' A lot of people hear. They listen . . . 'Do you have a favorite author, Sally Ann asks. 'Right!' I say. 'One'. It's for the listeners just as it's for Sally Ann . . . my favorite author comes from my father's set of leather bound books that he left . . . William Blake! 'He wrote a lot about Las Vegas,' I tell Sally Ann. She says she's heard of him. 'He's supposed to be interesting.' I quote from I Saw a Chapel All of Gold. 'This guy did everything,' I tell her: 'wrote; drew.' I don't like this group.*

The sense of alienation, of being part of the scene and at the same time not in the scene, comes through in other stories by Kranes. They are quite slight but suggestive of deeper emotional currents in the gambling life. In his novel *Keno Runner* (1989) Kranes gives these themes much richer and fuller treatment. It is a novel of discovery, of uncovering of the self which conveys, in a wholly original and imaginative way, the essential experience of Vegas.

In outline *Keno Runner* is about a writer who leaves a broken affair in New York to go to Las Vegas. He has a project to write a book about a young woman, Janice Stewart, who has been acquitted of a bizarre arson-murder charge in another state. She is working as a keno runner.[4] Within that brief frame, the characters undergo a profound transformation, in which Las Vegas is the catalyst.

Before flying to Las Vegas, however, the writer, who is named Benjamin Kohlman, stops off in Iowa to revisit the farm community where he grew up – a brief but significant detour.

> *. . . he stood there, dry and sweating, as he had done sometimes as a young man, when he ran: breathing heavily. And then did a crazy thing! He bent and swept dusty nuggets of earth up with a slap of his hand and stuffed them into his mouth and swallowed them. It was an act too late to reverse.*

It is only a brief moment, but sufficient. In *Keno Runner*, there is a presence, distant but actual, all the way through of the other, real America, behind the lights of Vegas, in the random postcards Kohlman receives from his parents, travelling America in a camper. A sense of slick urban New York is half present too, in the sharp ironic put-downs he receives from his former lover, who has turned him out.

The keno runner herself, Janice Stewart, turns out to be a

[4]Keno is a gambling game using cards with numbered squares.

mysterious young woman; fey, apparitional, other-worldly. Janice has the nickname of Angel because she once passed out, almost died, and came back but there is, it emerges, nothing weak about her. She is committed to life, and she soon becomes committed to Kohlman. She is the best keno runner, always on the go, and she loves her job. In an evocative and poetic confession (Kranes' writing excels in this combination of lightness and intensity) she sums up her role at keno.

> *I bring the numbers! . . . I bring the one-spots and the three-spots. And all the four and five-way combinations. I carry 63s! And 39s! and 4s! And 16s, 17s, and 18s – all in my hand! I carry 52s! I carry 80s! I carry 3s and 2s and 1s! I take them all! Old women in wheelchairs. Truckers. Marketing executives. Mad handkerchief-chewing women in shawls. Junkies. Murderers. I find them all! I take them I move for them. I bring them back. I bring the numbers from the numbers to the numbers! And I bring them back! I watch them watching . . . and I feel each light! All numbers. And all the numbers reaching even before number. Before word.*

Janice chooses to interpret her agreement to talk to Kohlman about her case as giving her life to him . . . as a marriage contract. "I gave you my life exclusively. It's a beautiful contract. You have me. It's on paper. We both signed." In vain Kohlman protests. Their roles reverse. Janice plies him with questions, demanding more and more of his time. Kohlman is drawn into her nimbus. He tries to explain it is only a book contract. He loses any sense of outline or direction for the work he is planning about her. He seems to be falling in love with her.

It is surreal, the experience he undergoes, and the Las Vegas all around them is surreal too. In a compelling dream-like series of scenes, reality is heightened, as it is in dreams. Everything is there, the casinos, the light, the hype, the hustle, even the boxing – but expressed indirectly, in tangential experiences, arising from the encounters and relationship of the two leading characters. The story, it transpires, has become Kohlman's quest for survival.

Take this very funny, accurate, real but unreal episode (among my favourites in the book) when Kohlman drifts into the Riviera:

> *He sat down at an empty blackjack table. The dealer nodded.*
>
> *A smiling man in a pewter-colored suit moved from the pit to the table. He stuck his hand out to Kohlman. "Mr. B!" he said. "Finally back! How's the war?"*
>
> *Kohlman shook the man's hand. Mr. B? . . . "Fine," he said.*
>
> *"We haven't seen you!" the pit boss said.*
>
> *"No," Kohlman said.*
>
> *"You've been away."*
>
> *"Yes."*
>
> *The pit boss put a hand on the dealer's shoulder.*
>
> *"Start Mr. B with a mark of two, Lonnie." Then he looked up at Kohlman: "Two – Mr. B? Am I on target? Did I remember?"*
>
> *"Fine," Kohlman said. He had no idea what was being transacted.*
>
> *"Standard fare," the pit boss said to Lonnie, the dealer.*

"Whenever you see Mr. B – start him off with a mark of two."

Things were happening. Kohlman was watching. Something was being filled out on a voucher pad. The dealer was gathering stacks of chips from his tray, lining them up, counting them, restacking them, lining them up again, counting. The pit boss pushed the voucher pad to Kohlman, handed over his pen. Kohlman hesitated, then scratched a signature where the man had indicated on the pad. The pit boss took the pad back, smiled at Kohlman, touched his own vest. "Jerry Lissac, Mr. B. I know I should've reminded you."

In fifteen minutes Kohlman more than triples his original chips. He asks the dealer how much he has. Lonnie eyeballs the stacks. Eighty-six hundred. Kohlman felt his mind go to white turbulence. His chips were hundreds, not as he assumed, dollars.

"Would you like to cash in your mark, sir – Mr. B?" Lonnie said.

"Sure," Kohlman said. "Right. That's a good idea. Cash in my mark."

Lonnie gathered all the chips and rearranged them. He drew off four stacks of five, separated them back towards his tray. He produced the voucher that Kohlman had signed. "Do you want to rip this up yourself? Or should I?" he said.

"Oh . . . go ahead," Kohlman said, "Rip. Fine."

Lonnie ripped the voucher. He set the chips he'd separated back into the tray. "Should I change these up for you?" he asked.

"Sure," Kohlman said. He felt lunatic. He felt buoyant, absolutely outside any laws of logic. Kohlman handed the black chip back. "Thank you," he said.

"Thank you, Mr. B."

Jerry Lissac was on the scene as Kohlman rose. "God, you did it to us again, Mr.B," he said to Kohlman.

"Well . . ."

"What can we get you? What can we do? How can we be there for you? It's ten minutes past nine: breakfast?"

This kind of vignette touches the quick of Las Vegas: its style, its mode of language, the casino experience, the transaction in its essence. Its hilarious clinching last two lines. But gambling is not what *Keno Runner* is about.

The story darkens: threats are made to Kohlman's life – mysterious people mistake his motives, confusing the arson he is talking about in Janice's earlier life with the investigation of a fire in Vegas. In these dream-like images of coloured violence, he is assaulted, shot at, cut, wounded, but never more than momentarily hurt. He survives and he discovers himself as he meets other, larger-than-life characters, friends, strangers, even the President of the United States.

Keno Runner presents Vegas more as a context, a confluence of strange forces – too bright, too vibrant, by turns indulgent and violent, extrovert yet introspective – than as a gambling resort. In its clear, sharp, disjointed style, its alternation between love and violence, Vegas becomes a wildly comic place, in control, out of control, an allegory of America. "Las Vegas isn't America . . . America is Las Vegas," Janice says at one point.

A surrealist film by Buñuel conveys something of the same rich, coloured, disturbing experience. As a work of imagination *Keno Runner* cannot be reduced to a simple formula. It ends in a multiple wedding of the leading characters, including Kohlman and Janice. And standing silently in the background, in significant witness, are Kohlman's parents, who have finally arrived.

One of the characters offers a clue to the strangeness of *Keno Runner.* It is just a fiction, with a happy ending. It has "No Basis in Daily Life as We Live It . . . No basis in the Bright Lights and Big City of our Working World." The book is subtitled 'a romance' and that, probably, is how it should be read.

All fiction about gambling tends to be a process of self discovery by the leading character. In the end *Keno Runner* is upbeat. It leaves Kohlman "More alive than he'd been since he'd been a child. He could *feel* it – himself, his own blood coursing through him!" Harmony, the desert rose, leaves on a bus on her way to Reno, ever hopeful of starting a new life with a new admirer. The protagonist of *Fools Die* achieves a sort of wisdom – "I was surrounded by countless tables of chance and I was under no illusion. I knew now the single fact that no matter how carefully I planned, no matter how cunning I was, lies or good deeds done, I couldn't really win."

By contrast, Aleksey Ivanovich, the hero of *The Gambler*, is not redeemed or purged. At the end of the story he is even more passionate in his obsession. "All I need to do is to be careful and prudent, just once in my life – that's all! All I have to do is keep control of myself for once, and I can change my whole destiny in one hour! The most important thing is strength of character." And he recalls how in Roulettenberg after he had lost everything, he found one gulden in his waistcoat pocket. He turned back to the casino and bet it, his very last coin, and won.

"But what if I had lost heart, if I had not dared to make that decision?" Tomorrow, he tells himself, he will rise up again, it will all come right.

Well, that is how all gamblers feel, whether in Roulettenberg or in Vegas. It is easy to write about Las Vegas, as an abundance of bad journalism proves. The reason is that Las Vegas makes a tremendously powerful onslaught on the senses of everybody who goes there, and at the same time poses a challenge to everyone's normal values. It insists on the basic questions – What do we feel about money? Or the kind of life in which money is the sole measurement of success? – while celebrating its own abnormality in a package of fun, designed to undermine self-questioning and moral judgement.

It is a place, to cite a formula of my own (in *All Right, Okay, You Win*, 1993), which is both wonderful and awful at the same time. That may be why writers who have sought to define its true nature have found it so elusive.

7

Mood Music in the World Championship

The only player who can beat me is myself
Stu Ungar, three-times world champion

Oh to be in Vegas, now that April's there! It is every poker player's dream, one day, to play in the World Championship. The tournament is held each year at Binion's Horseshoe in Las Vegas, down in Glitter Gulch. The event runs over four gruelling days, as the climax of Binion's month-long 'World Series of Poker'. The attraction is not (for me) the prospect of winning first prize of $1,000,000 – which as an amateur player, of modest talent, one can rule out in advance. It is the thrill of competing in what everyone recognizes as the most exciting and dramatic game of poker, anywhere in the world.

I never expected to do it, to have that pleasure, though it is quite feasible to gain the $10,000 entry fee by winning a satellite or, even more cheaply, a super-satellite. (In the former, ten players sit down at the table, putting up $1,000 each, and the winner scoops his entry fee; in a super-satellite up to a couple of hundred players pay a minimal entry fee of a mere $200, which produces, with rebuys, a pool large enough to stake half a dozen winning entries.) I did not have to go through all this, however.

A generous friend, with whom I play every week in an itty-bitty little home-town game – let me name him, George Hacker, what a guy! – decided to back me. George had a somewhat inflated idea of my ability, from observing my play aboard a poker cruise we took together in the Caribbean. (One does run around the world, via poker.) The money, to him, was not paramount. Still, no one had shelled out greenbacks for me in such quantity before in my life!

My experience of the World Championship was shattering. Of course, I couldn't do it justice in *The Independent*, the newspaper I write for – not as it actually happened, in all its gory detail. I wrote a preview of my hopes in my poker column, on May 15, 1997.

"I have about as much chance of winning the event, which is no-limit Texas Hold 'em, as of beating Tiger Woods at golf," I wrote. *"But that is not the point. What counts is the thrill and experience of competing against so many great players, including a whole raft of world champions. What's more anyone can get lucky, which in this event means catching a few good hands at the right moment."*

I continued: *"'You may be a 100 to 1 shot,'" the enthusiastic and talented Vegas pro Annie Duke encouraged me, "'but that means that once in 100 times you're gonna win!'"* I have seen too many friends crash in the World Championship to have any such illusions. One year, a player went out in the very first hand – he hit four aces and came up against a straight flush! No disgrace, but so painful.

My fellow poker writer Al Alvarez got trapped on a pair of queens early on when he played, and Tony Holden had aces wired outdrawn by a lucky flush to finish in 111th place. "I reeled away badly winded," he recalls in *Big Deal*, "as if I'd been punched hard in the stomach – a real physical pain, gradually giving way to a deep spiritual bruise."

My objective, I concluded, was a modest one. I wanted to survive the first session and if possible the first day. My intention was to follow a policy of 'selective aggression', i.e. playing very few hands but playing them hard, as recommended by Tom McEvoy in *Tournament Poker*. I might crash out, but I intended to give it my best shot. If I got through to the second day, that would be time enough to consider my game plan. Fortunately, I reasoned, there was a ready cure for being busted – move over to a new game as fast as possible!

Let's skip my arrival in Vegas and cut to the chase. One thing which novice entrants to the World Championship do not lack is advice. Stewart Reuben, a pro and probably one of the best two or three players in England, said: (a) you have no chance, (b) just play aces and kings wired and nothing else. Frank Thompson, a Yorkshire lad and now one of the established players at the Mirage, agreed: (a) you have no chance, (b) play pairs in the hole – you might get trips now and then. On the eve of battle, Richard Sparks, an old friend from down-home games in London, bought me a Chinese dinner to pep me up. Sounding like the ghost in Hamlet, he admonished me:

"Remember this! Hold 'em is a game of situations, not cards!"

On the morning of the great day Tony Holden, who had himself played three times in the event in past years, took on the role of manager.

Tony: "Relax! Go to your room!"

Me: "Sure, I've got a couple of Asian babes waiting up there."

Tony: "Okay, but only the one!"

In sober reality, I had a swim in the rooftop pool and then a modest breakfast. Down in the playing hall, which was Binion's old valet parking space now transformed to a vast white tent under a canvas canopy, scores of players were milling around, waiting for the off. Earlier I had cashed in $10,000 in traveller's cheques for my entry fee.

This in itself was a strange experience. Ten thousand bucks is quite a lot of money, which most of us would scrimp and save to get together. Cashing in the cheques required an extensive process of countersigning and then verification via telephone by the cashier. Finally the transaction was approved and then – anti-climax – she dropped into my hand seven pathetic little plastic buttons, known as casino chips. Holding them in my palm and then handing them over to the tournament desk, the chips seemed like tiddlywinks, not money at all. I began to see how professional players could treat the enormous sums they gambled with so lightly.

The draw for places and tables was broadcast over a loudspeaker by tournament director Jack McClellan. Jack Binion, owner of the joint and long-standing backer of the World Series, came to the mike to pronounce the time-honoured phrase: "Shuffle up and deal!"

I was at a good table right in the corner, away from the smoke. No world champions or other celebrities. On my immediate right was Yosh Nakano, a very well known pro and a friendly little man whom I knew slightly. On my left was a pencil-slim dude in a cowboy shirt with a slicked-back coiff of hair, like a 60s rocker. First thing, before a card was dealt, he made a pronouncement to the table, in a twanging Texan drawl,

"Ah took the lie de-tector, and the man sayed he had never seen such a PERFEC' result!"

Through the next hour, this fellow regaled the table at large with his story, which focused on a gal in the swimmin' pool, a party, a lot of drinkin' an' foolin' around, goin' inside the house to sleep, then someone or other breakin' in, the woman wakin' up 'n puttin' her arm through a glass patio door and cuttin' hersel' real bad, lots of *BLUHD*, the guy calling an ambulance, and so on. I tried to block it out. I wasn't feeling nervous, but made a weak start.

On the very first hand, sitting on the small blind with A-7, I decided not to get involved, and the flop came down with an A-7 on board. Was I, I wondered, playing only aces and kings wired or what? This indecision was just a touch unsettling. On my right, Yosh had taken out a tiny mobile phone. "I wan' a dime on the Lakers," I heard him say, "'n a dime on the Jazz." A dime, I realized, was a thousand dollar bet. "What is the balance of my account last week?" he enquired, as he casually threw in a small raise. His basketball action put the poker game in a new perspective. (He told me later he won.)

Another, darker melody was being played out here, like a counterpoint to the main theme. A group of half a dozen players from the Grosvenor Victoria casino in London had arrived in Vegas on an all-expenses paid trip, which was the prize – and how hard they fought for it! – each of them had won in little Saturday night tournaments back home. These players, all well known to me, were a friendly, hopeful bunch, but in the reality of poker, *losers*. I do not mean they could never win but over the weeks and months, they were losing players (as most club players are) and, more to the point now, they had no money left. They had scrimped and saved and gambled to raise a few hundred bucks to afford to play and make a go of their stay in Vegas, and they had already more or less lost their stake on their first twenty-four hours in town. I had not boasted about my own good fortune in getting a free entry to the World Championship, but everyone knew about it.

These guys looked on enviously from the rail, wishing they were playing. I wasn't worried about them because what they did or didn't do was of no concern to me; but I was anxious about one of them, Ronny, a good friend who sometimes tipped me horses. Ronny, who came from Singapore and had various gambling connexions out there still, was in fact a good poker player, but had a notorious dice habit. This 'leak' swallowed up all his winnings at poker, horse racing and everything else. I had sworn to myself, before leaving home, that come what may I would not lend Ronny money in Vegas. I wasn't sure now, looking at his eager, mournful face, that I would be able to stick to it.

In this opening session of the Championship, the blinds cost merely $25 and $50, which meant that, in theory, I could play all through the session, at say 30 rounds an hour, if I chose, without the risk of being busted out. The blinds would rise every two hours, culminating at the end of the tournament in antes of $2,000 a player and $10,000 – $20,000 blinds. At that rate, players could not sit back, they *had* to play. But at this opening stage there was very little action while the players were feeling each other out.

When I got aces wired, I bet five hundred, and flopped another ace. I knew if I bet, my opponent would fold, so I checked. Down came a third spade. Weakly, I checked again. The river card brought a fourth spade. I had the ace of spades and bet $600 and took the pot. This was very poor play. Better to bet the aces early, hoping my opponent had a hand, and if not, win the pot then and there. The first two hours seemed to take forever. When a break was called I had $9,975.

The blinds in the next session were raised to $50 – $100. The action was still tentative. I played 9s wired on the big blind and the flop came down 9-10-J, to give me a set, but with two diamonds on board. Again, I checked nervously – this was a very dangerous hand – hoping to get a free card and pair the board for a full house. Instead, another diamond flopped. The opener bet and I folded. The last player called on a straight to find a diamond flush out against him. So my cautious play was possibly correct.

If I had bet the trips on the flop, though, would the opener have called? Certainly an aggressive player would have bet my hand. This is the kind of thing you ponder while the next deal is coming down. (Later I heard from the rail, "Hey, David had to fold a big hand against a flush, bad beat!") At the end of this second two hours, which again felt agonizingly drawn out, I still had $9,000. No one at the table had made much progress. It was five o'clock in the afternoon, and I felt ravenous. Just time to gulp down a bowl of scalding broth at the snack bar and race back to the table.

Another theme, like a base below the main melody,

came in now, which in a way touches the core of the Vegas experience for me. How can I describe it? It's the music, really the discord, that subsists in the gap between what you feel and what you tell your friends back home.

It's like this: when you tell people from London or some other distant place that you are going to Las Vegas, their eyes light up. They are excited for you, they want you to do well – and they want to hear that you did well when you get back. You, or I, do not want to disappoint them. But the actual experience of Vegas is not a simple win-or-lose thing. It is complicated, tense, sometimes euphoric and often bitter and painful. Vegas is a place, as I wrote in my book *Welcome to the Pleasuredome*,[1] where you go not to get-away-from-it-all, but to feel-it-all-more-intensely. It is a place which, paradoxically, makes you focus back on your inner self, which leads to self-questioning in the middle of the night.

Why? As I say, it's not just a question of winning or losing money. I have both won and lost in Vegas on my many occasions, though never more than a couple of thousand bucks or so either way. It is more the realization that comes from playing poker (or gambling) so intensely, of one's limitations, of one's possibilities and of one's achievements, in life as well as in the game. That is why so much of the writing about Vegas is dark, downbeat and confessional in tone. Maybe the permanent residents get over all that, but they must surely go through it when they first move to town.

[1] I can't resist quoting my favourite review, by the late, great Bill 'Bulldog' Sykes, which lauded the book and nicely punctured my pomposity. "This Spanier fellow is one smart cookie. He's done just about everything but check-raise with a royal flush and have an affair with the queen."

On this trip, I was assailed by the usual qualms. I began losing – only small amounts, like $250 or $300. I was not going to miss a meal (nearly everything was comped at Binion's anyway) or even feel such minimal losses, which were obviously irrelevant to my life from a financial point of view. (I had brought adequate reserves.)

It was rather a feeling, which all true poker players have, of letting yourself down, of playing badly. Winning or losing in itself, in the short term, is not important. What matters is playing correctly. These little limit-raise games are quite tough on us British players who are used to the smash-and-grab of pot limit. In limit games you try and make one extra bet or save one extra bet in the hand, and all the dynamics of play are different. I knew all that, naturally, and could play the game properly. But still . . . my losses could not be attributed to bad cards or outdraws. When I lose at poker – and this is an article of faith with me – it is not because (except in rare cases) of bad cards. It is because I played badly!

The pattern of my days was to get up early (never can sleep in this town), take a swim, join the game mid-morning, play for two or three hours depending on the run of the game, have a snacky lunch with any friend who happened to be around, sometimes have an interview with a casino manager as part of my journalism, try to take a nap in the afternoon, play a couple of hours again before dinner, go out for a stupendous, bibulous meal somewhere, and return about midnight to play two or three more hours or however long I felt like it through the night.

Sometimes we Brits would play at the same table, jokily,

enjoying the irony – "*Hi' hyand!*" we would cry, the word high extending to an elongated cowboy wail *"Ha-i-i-i!"* – outdoing the local yokels in their own accents. One should never play when drunk. On the other hand, I maintain that Texas Hold 'em is the only poker game you can play when you feel a little flown with wine – because (unlike stud) there are only two cards to remember. Yeah, well, that is what I like to think.

So I suppose I'm talking about mood swings. To be up a few hundred feels good. To be down a few hundred dollars is not serious in money terms, but feels bad, very bad. One begins to suspect a losing trend and then wake up at 4 a.m. after a couple of hours' fitful sleep to calculate on the back of an envelope how much money I have left, how much I can risk each day – $500 or $550? – for the rest of the trip – or (calamity) whether I might have to borrow from a friend. Which is never quite as easy as it sounds, especially in Vegas, far from home.

Of course Suzy and I talked every day, at home in London or from Paris – to win at poker, your wife needs to be happy, I believe. The time difference and distance, however, made conversation about Vegas, or anything else, virtually impossible.

A mood of elation one day swings to doom-and-gloom the next. That is what you get in Vegas, an emotional switchback every damn day. I could tell it was the same sort of thing for the Victoria casino players from London. Every time I ran into one of them I would ask: "How's it going?" They would shrug or raise their eyebrows in mock helplessness. "These limit-raise games . . . what a farce." I knew they were broke to a man – none more so than Ronny.

"I played dice the first night, it was a disaster." He laughed in despair at himself. "What a disaster!" "You'll get it back, Ronny," I told him, without conviction.

Another incident happened, which in a way was trivial but which upset me nevertheless. I ran into another player I knew from way back somewhere and couldn't remember his name. This is always slightly embarrassing because such people always know who I am, simply because I have written a book about poker. To such people I probably do seem a mini-celebrity. So I hate not to know who they are when they speak to me familiarly, as this man did. He was playing in a small game and I sat behind his chair, racking my brains as to who he was.

Finally I came out with: "Listen I'm terribly sorry, I'm so tired, will you remind me of your name?" And this guy, aged about fifty with short grizzled hair and a lived-in look, took terrible offence. I sensed a major row about to blow up.

"Perhaps you knew my wife better?" he inquired savagely.

"Oh, um," I stammered. "How is your wife?" hoping to get some handle on the name.

"She's dead."

I fled to the poker tent looking for a player from back home who might know who this fellow was. Lucy Rokach came back with me to the game. The man had gone. Then I sort of got it, seeing him standing at the side, and remembered him. I had played with him and his wife, who had died, the rumour was had been murdered, a year ago. I ran up to the man and embraced him with both arms and he hugged me back.

"Of course I remember you!" I apologised. "You've

shaved off your beard, that's all!" This close encounter also revealed that he was a good way towards being drunk. "Let's go to the bar," I suggested. I ordered him a whisky sour. The tenor of our conversation can be judged from its opening exchange.

"What are you doing these days?"

"Waiting for death."

Yes, indeed, we're all doing that. We had another drink and I managed to extricate myself.

The switchback of moods came again, having dinner at Morton's that night with Frank Thompson. Frank has never quite lost the alert, round-eyed look of an out-of-town visitor, gazing around at the wonders of Vegas, despite the hard grind of the poker circuit. He is years younger than me, in fact I have known him since he first started out in the card clubs back in London. But where he has long been an established pro, competing against all-comers for high stakes, I have remained an amateur. He regards me, indulgently, as what is known in poker parlance as 'weak-tight' and he may be right.

Frank was talking about the game they had been playing at the Mirage, which was \$300-\$600 stud. That is, raises of \$300 up to card five and \$600 from card five on. In other words, one single opening bet was equivalent to the whole of one of my own paltry losing sessions! I accepted that I would never, ever, be able to play that sort of game, even with George's money. I knew that already, but it still rankled.

My mood was not improved when I ordered, at this very pretentious and expensive steak house, reputedly the best in Vegas, a vegetable platter, and was served huge clumps of over-boiled broccoli. If there is one thing that turns me off about Vegas it is that you cannot get a simple green salad such as you could find in any little café the length and breadth of France.

By late afternoon on the first day, the rhythm of the championship had imposed itself and I felt more settled. The betting had risen, the Texan on my left had exhausted his tale of crime and passion and was whining on about nuthin' in particular. To my surprise, I found aces wired again. I bet five hundred and the big blind called. The flop came down something like 3–4–8 off suit. He checked and, weakly, I checked along, hoping to trap him on the turn card. Terrible play, because the turn brought a 5. Now I did feel nervous of the flop. He bet $1,200 at me. I stopped to think. This bet was way above the level the table had been betting up to then and, first thought, I put it down to a bluff to run me out. On the big blind, I figured he might have played two low cards, for a straight draw, or had a low pair with a straight draw. He knew I was nervous and, if not an absolute beginner, certainly a rank amateur.

I did not want to pay $1,200, about a fifth of my stack, and face another big bet on the river. He wore dark spectacles which he took off from time to time when he bet. I folded. Afterwards, and when I say afterwards I mean forever and a day afterwards, I berated my weak play. I should have bet the aces, should have called or, better yet, raised him $1,200 back. Put the heat on *him*. These are the might-have-beens of the World Championship, turning points between winning a pot on the way to survival or going down without a fight.

At the end of this session I still had about $7,500, which was all right to go on with. The Texan finally got busted, holding aces and kings against trip 9s, by a Norwegian player who showed by his taciturn aggression that he knew what he was doing. The guy who had made me put down aces did not last long either, which was some satisfaction. The table was reduced to six and with an hour to go, we were moved.

I found myself at the opposite end of the tent at a table with former world champion Doyle Brunson and half a dozen other players all of whom had $15,000–$20,000 in chips compared with my meagre stack. I was too nervous to greet Brunson, as I so easily and flatteringly could have done, since his photograph adorned the jacket of my recently reprinted paperback of *Total Poker.* Nor did I recognize a lady at the table who was, of all things, a kalooki player from the Vic in London. She had a mound of chips too.

I was curious to see how Brunson played. Sure enough, on the first hand he was in, he called a small bet to a flop of A-2-6 and hit a magical 4 to make a low straight. Then he checked his hand against two 6s showing on the river, and won the hand with a pair of aces in the hole! Clearly, this was not a guy you could easily read.

Meanwhile the antes went around at $25 each player with $100 and $200 blinds.

With about $5,700 in chips, I calculated I could last four or five rounds before I had to make a move. I picked up the blinds, which gave me more breathing space.

There was about an hour to go before close of play for the first day – the first real test of survival. I knew I wanted to get there with, if possible, about $20,000. I reckoned that to come through with only half my starting stake, say under $5,000, would be tantamount to failure, since I would still have to double through almost immediately to survive at the next level of blinds on the second day's play.

So with about half an hour to go, I found jacks wired in the hole on the small blind. Everyone folded round to me and I decided just to call on the big blind. I wanted him to bet, so I could raise him back and double my $5,000. Down came a beautiful flop, so I thought – 10–8–7. I had a higher pair and a gutshot straight draw. I bet my $5,000, easily my biggest bet all day. He thought a moment and called me. He probably put me on K-10 or Q-10 or maybe a straight draw with a 9. The dealer burned and turned the cards. No nine for me, no jack, no pair, no improvement. I still thought I had won the hand, but he showed me 10–8 in the hole for two pairs. As I said in my poker column, Exit Dave. I stood up, my vision in a blur, and stumbled out of the hall. O-U-T spells out.

I didn't feel too bad at first, because I thought I had taken my best shot at survival. Not so! I called Frank Thompson who asked me what hand I went out on. When I told him, he immediately explained that I had misplayed it – badly. I had to bet the jacks *before* the flop! If I had bet all my chips I would have certainly won the antes, which would pay for another round. If I had made a smallish bet, say $1,000, would he have called? What for? As it was I simply gave my opponent a free draw to improve. He might have had the very worst starters at Hold 'em, 7–2 offsuit, and still hit something playable. Why give him that free roll?

As the realization sank in that I had misplayed the hand, and very badly at that, my spirits sank. Tony Holden was on the rail to offer his sympathy, which he did very generously. When he had played, he explained, there were only 180 players in it, not 312, so I had in effect survived far longer than he had done. He said all the right things, but the awful ache in the pit of my stomach did not go away.

One of the most famous stories about the world championship was the way the late, great 'Treetops' Jack Straus had won the title in 1982. He had fought his way back starting from a single $500 chip, which he had found under his cigarette pack. He had won the blinds, played it up, doubled through, and by good fortune and good judgement come right back into the event. Finally he had won the championship. I had blown it.

I wandered around aimlessly, took a walk around the block – it was still steamy hot outside – came back, sat down, had a glass of water and talked desultorily to a few friends, hurting all the time. It was now about 10.30 p.m., play had ended for the day and a crowd of happy triumphant players streamed out, all smiling and chattering, to go to the buffet upstairs. Donnacha O'Dea, whom I had consulted in London, was ebullient – he had $26,000, far more than he expected on the first night, which gave him a real chance. I could not possibly eat. I wanted to wait until 1 a.m. when I could call George in England and give him the bad news.

Finally, I swallowed an item described as a 'Binion Burger' as a kind of punishment, then I went up to my room and rang George. It was breakfast time in Gloucestershire. I tried to picture him brewing coffee, mulling over the morning papers, as I explained what had happened.

George was terrific. There were no it-might-have-beens or other post-mortems. "You did well," George insisted, "David, I'm proud of you!" That was a helluva nice thing to say, considering it was George's money that I had blown. I felt more grateful for his generosity of spirit, at that low point of my Vegas journey, than I could manage to mumble out. I did not feel proud of myself, in any way.

Next day, I had an unexpected reaction. I wanted to get out of Vegas, right away from it, the one place which, like a pilot light at the back of my mind, lit my hopes through the year. But I had to stay on and see the championship through, simply as a journalistic commitment. I rang the airline, at least to shorten my trip, but there were no seats on earlier flights – Vegas is always booked up. Besides I had an appointment to see the Mayor.

I don't know what kind of person you imagine would be Mayor of Las Vegas, city of hard-nosed casino managers and shadowy operators behind the scenes. Well, she was a chic-looking babe in a designer miniskirt, pendant earrings, flashy brooch and crimson nails straight out of Raymond Chandler. Sorry! I'll rephrase that. The Mayor, whose office is just a couple of blocks from the Horseshoe downtown, was a trim business-like person, in her late forties and extremely well briefed on all the civic issues of the day.

Mayor Jan Laferty Jones was now in her second four-year term. What was on her mind, I asked her, for an article I planned to write in my newspaper back in London? Las Vegas, she explained, was paying the price for its own huge success as the fastest growing city in America. What it needed, to break the gridlock in transportation, relieve the pressure on its educational and medical facilities and clean up environmental pollution, was cooperation by the casino operators, both on the Strip and Downtown. Unfortunately, in the business of turning a fast billion, none of them were prepared to stop, think and pull together. The Mayor, as Las Vegas' senior public official, the figurehead on the prow, was struggling to give a lead and foster collective action.

There was another side to Mayor Jones, which I think I can reveal without betraying any confidences. She was in the middle of a romantic entanglement whose outcome neither she nor her partner could foresee. Richard Schuetz was then running the Stratosphere. I had known Richard, one of the most talented managers in the casino business, for some years. He had given me a lot of help when I was researching my Vegas book. Really he was a 'people person', who seemed to enjoy a first-names relationship with all of his hundreds of employees. He invited me to dinner at the revolving restaurant, 108 floors up in the 1,149 feet high Stratosphere Tower. Her Honour was also coming.

The Stratosphere was in fact doomed and Richard knew it. It was, in my estimation, a fabulous property – with a 360 degrees view of the city from the tower – but it had cost too much. What was crucially against it, however, was its location, in the middle of no man's land halfway between the Strip and Glitter Gulch. People could not or would not get out there. Richard had slashed his gaming margins, which had helped boost volume but not profits. Everyone in town knew that the place, already in chapter 11 bankruptcy, was going to be written off by its parent company and re-launched with new financial backing. The only reason Richard was staying on, and not bailing out of the great glass sphere of the Stratosphere while it was still airborne, was to show solidarity with his 3,400 staff.

He spent all day and all night suspended in this vast

bubble, where he kept an apartment, hardly venturing outside. He had originally met the Mayor when he called to discuss parking zones. One thing had led to another, as it so often does. Ms. Jones, too, beset by her struggles with casino executives, took refuge in the Stratosphere. She came to see Richard whenever she was off duty. After I whooshed up in the elevator to have dinner with Richard, she joined us. They were happy together, floating high in the Stratosphere, revolving slowly above the myriad lights of Las Vegas, suspended briefly from diurnal cares and far away from their jobs.

At the end of my interview in the Mayor's office, when we had finished discussing mundane matters like air and water and pollution, I felt bold enough to offer a vision of my own. "I see you and Richard," I told her, "in coloured parachutes, floating down from the top of the Stratosphere Tower, flying away to a new life with no hassles or hang-ups."

The Mayor smiled back. "I wish!" she said.

A year later, I read an article in the *Las Vegas Sun* by Richard Schuetz. "Like most men, I am not particularly good at remembering dates," he wrote. "But I will always remember January 3, 1998. This was the day I was told that the person dearest to my heart was suffering from cancer."

A week later they were married. "We did not know of the future we were facing, but we were certain we wanted to face it together." To say that his account of the couple's ordeal was inspiring would be to miss the point. The Mayor continued to perform her job and their life continued "with a depth of thought and emotion that was unimaginable" before this terrible blow. I am glad to report that Ms.

Jones survived and got well, evoking widespread regret when she decided against running for a third term. Their story puts losing a few hundred bucks here and there into perspective, I think.

Next afternoon, I ran into Ronny again. He was flat broke but cheerful. I wanted friendly company, and I was also curious to see how Ronny, an expert, a past master, so to speak, at being busted, was managing without money in this town which is fuelled day and night by money. He led me off to visit the stores at the end of the main casino block in Glitter Gulch, to look for track shoes for his son.

Potted palm trees had been set up along Fremont Street, radiating showers of spray, like fine mist, which passers-by could stand under to keep cool – a nice touch. The gimcrack little stores east of Fremont offered tee-shirts and caps and souvenirs, at cut prices for tourists who had any money left to spend. Ronny and I had been there on a previous trip when I had bought a San Diego cap because the initials S D were my own the other way round. Ronny could not find the brand of shoes he wanted, and decided against. Probably his credit card was not operable again until after midnight. That was how fine a line he played in raising cash for survival.

Then I had a bright idea. "Ever been to the Gambler's Book Club?" I asked. This was a must-stop point of call for me on every visit to Vegas. I hailed a taxi and out we went. The Gambler's Book Club, ten minutes away on South 11th Street, has every book on every sort of gambling you can think of. It is run by Howard Schwartz, who is a living compendium of gambling books and gambing lore, whom anyone writing on the subject always consults. The store is not big but has a lot of space out back, where Howard keeps old books, manuscripts and other memorabilia, and likes to gossip.

In the store the shelves are arranged under different games, roulette, poker, blackjack, and so on, with diverse sections on fiction, biography and gambling history. Under the dice section, I found a book called something like 'The Truth about Craps' and passed it to Ronny without comment.

Howard always has news and views of what's doing. Better yet, he always comes up with new ideas for me to write a book about. He loves to push and promote writers. He sells all the British authors on gambling and gets us to sign copies of our books.

This time Howard, who is a bachelor, a bibliophile and somewhat paranoiac (he always carries a spray can of Mace) was thrilled because he had found a stray cat, who had installed herself in the back of the store. She had had a litter of kittens, which he had managed to find homes for. The cat looked to me like a very scaredy-cat, as she swerved away from my presence, but Howard was happy with her, like a new lover.

"She's shy because she never goes out," he explained.

"Why not let her run around a bit?"

"She might get lost."

"So put an identity disc round her neck," I suggested.

He looked at me, astonished and indignant. "What! And have someone *blackmail* me for her return!" – pure Howard.

Ronny's nose was still in the dice book. "Let me buy that for you," I told him. "No, no, I don't want it." I bought it anyway. I was curious to see how Ronny was going to touch me for a loan, as I knew he would when he judged the moment was right – he is an artist in timing his borrowings. Probably that was why he had fallen in with me that afternoon.

As I had my wallet out to pay for the book, he said: "Let me pay for it, David. Just let me have a couple of hundred dollars, and I'll pay you back as soon as we get to London." Nice try!

"Ronny," I told him, "if you have any bills you have to pay, I'll pay them for you. Just give them to me. But I'm not giving you a dime to gamble with."

"No bills, no problems," Ronny said. We took a cab back to Binion's where the second day of the championship was under way.

To my surprise, our little visit to the Gambler's Book Club had changed my mood again. I felt my confidence flowing back like a spring tide coming in, cleansing me. I was busted out of the championship, but so what – I had expected to be busted. I felt almost okay again.

In the white poker tent the second day's play was in full spate. About 150 players were involved, who by the end of the night would be reduced to a final 27. They would all be 'in the money'. From 27th to 19th place, the finishers would pick up $21,200 dollars each, which was not all that much reward for their initial stake of ten grand. The prize money then rose progressively up to the last six places, who all got six figure pay-offs. They would comprise the coveted final table on the fourth and final day. The winner, who got a straight million, being accorded the title of World Champion.

A tradition of Binion's, highly esteemed by the poker fraternity, was that the winner of each event in the World Series was awarded a golden bracelet, inscribed with his name, recording his victory. You could usually spot such winners casually displaying their bracelets round their wrists as they picked up and played their cards.

At the other end of the white tent, cash games were roaring away, pot limit Hold 'em and Omaha, at stakes far higher, in immediate cost to the players, than the championship itself. The boys from the Victoria club in London who had started out playing these cash games, hoping to make a quick hit, were by now reduced to playing little $3-$6 limit-raise games in the casino card room. Or in Ronny's case, sitting patiently behind a friend and watching his play. I recalled a witty remark Ronny had made to me before the championship started: "David, if you had to take a written exam on this tournament, you would get a starred A, no problem!" Yeah, the practical was my problem.

As holder of a press pass I was allowed to wander around inside the arena, looking at the play of the hands. For a would-be high stakes player, this is a privilege as well as an education. I could sometimes peek at players' hole cards, from behind their cupped hands, and witness all manner of confrontations.

The general style of play at this stage was for a player to look for pairs of aces or kings (which are hard to come by) or A-K, sometimes A-Q or A-J, and stick all their chips in before the flop. The idea is to win the hand there and then, or force an opponent who wants to challenge the bet to take the worst of it. These plays are finely judged, because in a two-handed showdown a middling pair like 7–7 is about even money against A-K. At Hold 'em, position round the table is crucial. First to speak has the initiative but last to act usually has the advantage.

Obviously, too, there is a lot of luck in how the cards fall. The fascination of No-limit Hold 'em is how championship contenders, with their experience, their knowledge of their opponents, and above all their almost extrasensory awareness of what is going on around the table, tend to make more good plays than bad plays.

One mistake, at this stage of the tournament, is usually enough to be busted. The loser stands up, sometimes even before the final cards are dealt out, turns away, his or her face empty of expression behind blank eyes, and stumbles off. (If any poker player was 'waiting for death', this was it.) No one at the table says a word in commiseration – it may be their turn next. In fact they are pleased there is one less opponent to beat. Sometimes the winner exults in a very un-English way (bad form, old chap, what!) by leaping to his feet or punching the air. And the deal goes on. By dinner time there were about 80 players left. They started again at 10 p.m., it was going to be a late night.

Stu Ungar, the diminutive Vegas player, back-to-back winner of the championship in 1980 and '81, was looking very good. After a long period of turning on and dropping out since those dual victories, 'the Kid' was back. When the cameras came around, he donned a pair of blue-tinted John Lennon granny specs, which partly concealed his somewhat ravaged nose. As often happens in World Championships, the likely winner seems to establish his form and his dominance early on. This year Ungar looked the part.

I was sorry to see my Dublin friend Donnacha O'Dea fall by the wayside. He has a tremendous track record in the championship and if there was one player I would have backed to get in the money it would be Donn. He caught aces wired, and checked them to trap another British player, Mel Judah, who went all-in on a pair of nines. Now Donn was a huge favourite, but a third 9 came down. That is the risk you run of checking 'pocket rockets'.

About midnight, when there were 30-odd players vying for the 27 pay-off spots, the tournament organiser Jack McClelland asked if they would like to stop and re-start an hour earlier next day. One or two were against the move, so play continued. This is the most fraught moment of the championship, when players stand on the very edge of making it, seeing the promised land of the final table, not from a mountain top, but just across the room. When the championship gets down to 30 players, at three tables, the deals are synchronised to ensure everyone gets the same number of hands, rather than one table of players having to play more hands than another. At 28 players, the tension is intense. This position, if you lose, is known as being 'on the bubble', the worst result in the whole tournament.

Despite all his expertise, one man blew it. It happened this way: he had about $40,000 in chips, whereas several others held only a few thousand. So one of them could hardly avoid being busted out in a couple of hands' time, simply on the cumulative cost of the antes and blinds.

Yet this one player got so carried away in the ongoing battle he chose to commit all his chips against an opponent playing off a bigger stack – a classic mistake. Such an aggressive bet, all-in, meant that if the bettor lost the hand, he would be out of chips and out of the tournament; whereas his opponent, having more chips than he had, would still be there, still with chances, even if he lost. And the bettor's A-J was smashed by a high pair.

As this unfortunate player saw what he had done, he stood up, trembling, and fled the room, his face white. He was going to remember this mistake, this totally unnecessary mistake, not just that night and the next day, but all his life. Even if he had found a pair of aces in the hole, in that particular situation of being 'on the bubble', he should have thought twice before risking all his chips against a player with a bigger stack. He had an automatic win of $21,200 simply by sitting pat and not playing any hand at all, with the potential, next day, of going on to win a million.

Miserable as I was at my own performance, I would rather have gone out on the first hand than lost at this point. As the loser left the tent, the other players pushed their chairs back, relaxed, started laughing and joking in relief, joshing about all the hands they had just played or bluffed or drawn out on. The room was alive again. They were the happy 27, who would enter the third day with everything to play for.

I slipped away for dinner with a bunch of my fellow journalists and ordered a couple of bottles of wine. At the start of my stay I was scrupulous in paying for such items rather than signing them away on my press pass. By now, though, who cared about petty cash? – all of us signed for everything. What did another thirty or forty bucks on a comp matter when everyone around was gambling their heads off in hundreds and thousands?

Flown with wine, I sat down at midnight in a $15–$30 game and won a pot right off, which was a good omen. But the game was scrappy. On my left was a woman from Idaho who had finished as high as 31st in the championship and was clearly a capable player. On my right a man wearing a sports shirt and tennis shorts, as if he had just come off court, was continually bounding out of his seat and speeding around, coming back to play a couple of hands, and then running off again. The game, down to five or six players most of the night, was unsettling. I dropped another four or five hundred before hitting the sack at 3 a.m. Not serious, but I couldn't remember when I had last booked a decent win.

Which leads to that moment, that 'gap' I described earlier, between trying to square the experience you are actually having in Vegas (glittery dark) and what your family and friends back home want to hear (glittery bright). It's around 1 or 2 a.m. in Vegas when I ring Suzy in Paris or the boys at home.

"Hi Dad!" they cry. "How are you doing?"

"Great!" (Win some, lose some, would be a better answer, but feeble).

Suzy is wiser in poker ways. "You mean 'just about broke even'?" she says ironically, which she knows is poker parlance for losing.

"That's right. But I'm having a great time, great."

"Well, enjoy yourself!" and we go on to talk about family things.

The boys are not so easily satisfied. They wanted to know where I finished in the championship and what happened.

"I came 150th, got through the first day, almost."

"Does that mean you're the 150th best player in the world, Dad?"

"Yeah, well, not quite. Thereabouts, you could say," I fib.

"Tell us about the hands!"

My best story by far, which happened a while back, concerned Amarillo Slim, when he was dealing out hands in the press tournament. Slim was one of those characters from the early days of the championship whom everyone knew. After winning the title in 1972 he parlayed his talent as a wise crackin', easy goin', fast talkin' cowboy into becoming the most colourful character on the poker circuit. Six foot something and tall and thin as a beanpole, Slim wore a white stetson and cowboy boots and ambled around gamblin' and hustlin' and dispensing country-boy wisdom. The famous saying about losers, 'Nobody knows, where the hobo goes, when it snows', is attributed to him.

Anyway, Slim was taking a turn dealing in the press game, which is held the night before the World Championship, as a free-roll for the media. We were all speeding around on any old cards, so much so that I played hands like king-three off suit. On the flop down came a king. I bet and got a couple of callers.

"Three cowboys," drawled Slim, "who's got the hi' kicker?" He dealt the turn card and then the river (last) card, which was a three.

"If that trey helps anyone's hand," twanged Slim, "I'll piss in mah hat!" and he took off his Stetson and set it on the table.

"Well, actually, Slim," I declared in my cut-glass English accent, "I've got a three down here!"

'I'll piss in my hat' became a sort of family saying.

On this trip I hadn't got any stories to match that, but I sounded like a guy having a good time. Which I was, half the time.

Day three of the championship brought the last 27 players together. Some had great stacks of chips, like Stu Ungar with $232,000 in tournament chips, some were down to a few thousand and did not last long. Play would go on until there were six players left, who would make up the final table. There were three Irish players in, four Brits (one or two foreign-based players claimed British residence for tax reasons) and two Scandinavians – confirmation of a distinct tilt, this year, towards the Old World.

No tears were shed for Phil Hellmuth Jnr. a former champion, busted early on a pair of 8s. No question he is a great player, and a clear generation younger than the regular Vegas pros, but he has the kind of arrogance at the table, and not only at the table, which other players find obnoxious and don't know how to deal with. For instance, from time to time he will suddenly flop down on his back, stretched full length on the floor beside his chair, eyes closed, headphones on, supposedly relaxing.

Ungar was playing well, calling a big bet from a king showing and winning on a pair of 9s, and later bluffing out a pair of 9s with only a king high himself. He has, it is generally recognised, a fantastic feel for cards. In his younger days, growing up in Manhattan, he had a reputation as the best gin rummy player in America.

The final next day was staged outdoors, an innovation, in a kind of boxing ring erected on Fremont Street. It was hot, close to a hundred degrees, but not too oppressive at 10 a.m. when play started. The chief worry was whether the desert wind might blow the cards around. Ungar was in the lead with $1,660,000 in chips.

Around noon, our group of press moved inside to watch the play on big TV monitors in the tent, over a few drinks.

Stu won, as expected. He seemed pleased but didn't look all that thrilled, behind his blue specs. In the traditional climax to the World Championship, security men carried in a cardboard box, an old soap carton as it happened, containing a million dollars in bundles of ten thousand, which they strewed around the table for the photographers. As the event was being staged outside, could someone stage a heist via a helicopter? Not with all those armed guards around.

After it was over Jack Binion threw a buffet on Fremont Street for the players and press and assorted hangers-on, which made a merry conclusion to the event. I was having dinner with Frank Thompson and his girlfriend later, and began to feel really in the mood for Vegas. Now I felt sorry that I couldn't delay my flight and stay through the weekend.

The raggle-taggle band of players from the Victoria were also preparing to leave town. They waited by the check-out desk at Binion's, scrabbling through their pockets to find a last few dollars for a mini-cab to the airport. They looked like the remnants of Napoleon's army on the retreat from Moscow, if you can imagine such a scene in hot weather.

Here is the report on my effort, as it appeared in my poker column in *The Independent* on May 29, 1997.

I returned to London after playing in the World Championship at Binion's Horseshoe in Las Vegas very much richer. Richer, that is, in experience rather than greenbacks. Everyone should enter the event once in their lives. The championship is an intense emotional experience because everyone involved – this year there were 312 entrants paying $10,000 each – knows it is the biggest deal in poker. Fourteen former world champions were competing and an array of top class American and international players.

What can I tell you? I lasted until almost the end of

the first day, by which time 150 entrants had been busted out. I played badly, mainly in not pushing my good hands hard enough. If the eventual winner, Stu Ungar, had had my cards, I have no doubt he would have been $10,000 ahead, rather than $10,000 down, on the first night. The physical drive of the event is relentless. On the first day we played four two-hour sessions, with a fifteen-minute break between them, which is only just long enough to make it to the loo. On the second day, when the field was reduced to 27, the players were in action for over twelve hours. One slip is enough to ruin your chances.

When a player is busted, he simply stands up and quits the table. No one looks up, no one has time to commiserate. He or she feels simply terrible, but that is the downside of competing. After a day or two, the shock and the pain wear off. Hey! At the end of the championship 300 or so other players all feel bad, too. 'Bad beat city' is my nickname for Las Vegas.

Here is my final hand. Sitting on the little blind, everyone folded round to me. I found ***J-J*** *wired. I decided to try and double through on my remaining $5,000 in chips, and checked to the big blind. (I should have bet, to win the antes, not give him a free draw!) Down came what I thought was a dream flop:* ***10–8–7****, giving me a higher pair and a gutshot straight draw. I bet my stack and after some thought he called. He showed* ***10–8*** *which stood up. Exit Dave.*

Appendix

Hold 'em Basics

Hours of boredom and moments of terror
– Player's description of No-limit

I have more or less taken it for granted that everyone knows how to play Hold 'em but just in case some readers don't know the game, which is mentioned so frequently in my text, a short explanation may be useful.

Texas Hold 'em, as it is known by its full name, is the most popular game in modern poker. It is played in all the card rooms across the United States and in Europe, and is the game of the World Championship.

On the face of it, Hold 'em looks simple. Just two cards in the hole (dealt face-down to each player) and five cards dealt face-up in common. In fact it is an extremely subtle game, marked by fast action and strong betting and characterised by an unusual if not unique *positional* factor.

As its name implies, the game came out of Texas and the South-West, where men are men, and not afraid to gamble. The name Hold 'em perhaps derives from players yelling 'Hold 'em!' at the dealer to stop a card coming down which might break their hand. The game requires judgement and courage in about equal measure, and attracts pros and amateurs alike.

At Hold 'em, players receive *two cards* in the hole, followed by five cards dealt out in common.

(x-x) player's hand /	**xxx 'the flop' /**	**x 'the turn' /**	**x 'the river'**
1st bet	**2nd bet**	**3rd bet**	**last bet**

After the hands are dealt, the first three cards dealt together face-up are called *'the flop'*. A fourth card, known as *'the turn'* and a fifth card called *'the river'* (as in down the river) also face-up, follow. There is a betting round at each stage.

Within this simple framework, of a hand of just two cards plus five community cards, there is scope – surprisingly enough – for much art and craft, or shall we say judgement and bluff. Players may use either or both their hole cards with the cards in common to make their final poker hand of five cards; or on occasion, all five up-cards without support of a hole card.

Here is an example of a Hold 'em deal (as illustrated in *Hold 'em Poker* cited below):

A **A♣ 10♦**　　B **A♦ Q♠**
Flop **A♠ 10♥ 8♥** Turn **7♦** River **3♥**
D **A♥ 7♥**　　C **6♦ 9♦**

Player A's best hand is **A A 10 10 8**
B's 〃 〃 **A A Q 10 8**
C's 〃 〃 **6 7 8 9 10**
D's 〃 〃 **A 10 8 7 3** heart flush

Before the cards are dealt, there are normally two 'blind' bets in Hold 'em, which are like the antes in other games. The player who is sitting to the left of the dealer puts up the *small blind*, which is an obligatory forced opening bet, say $1 or $2, or maybe $20 or $50 or a $100, depending on the size of the game; and the player to his left puts up the *big blind* which is double the first bet. These two bets constitute the initial pot.

Then each player round the table in turn can either call or raise the big blind but if he doesn't like his hand, he cannot just check it. In this opening round, if a player doesn't want to call the bet made by the big blind, he has to fold.

When the betting comes all the way round to the two players who had to post the small and big blinds, they in turn have the option of calling any raises or, if they want, re-raising.

In subsequent rounds, the betting always starts with the player to the left of the dealer who is on *the button*. A buck, or little round marker ('the buck stops here'), signifies the button, which is moved round one place to the left after each deal. So all the players have to post the blinds in turn.

0 Dealer
J **A** small blind
H **B** big blind
G **C** first to speak
F **D**
E

The intricacy of the game comes from the positional factor. It makes a huge difference if you are next to the dealer and first to act, or sitting halfway round the table, or last to act – in a full table 10, or even 11 can play.

In early position, a player needs high cards to open (a high pair or ace plus a face card or two high-suited or straightening cards) because of the risk of being raised by a player in a later position (with a stronger hand).

As the initiative moves around the table, each player has to make up his (or her) mind if the pot justifies a call or a raise, depending on his own hand, his position and his assessment of what's going on.

In last position, for example, if no one can raise behind you, a player might find it worth playing on almost anything, even **7–2** off-suit, the worst hand at Hold 'em (because it cannot improve on the flop to either a straight or a flush). Who knows? – the flop might come down **7–7–2**.

The cards in common mean that play is often very finely shaded. For example, who wins the following hand?

A: **A♣ J♥**
Flop: **A♠ Q♦ 9♦ 4♠ 9♠**
B: **A♦ 8♦**

Answer: it's a *split* pot, two pairs aces and 9s with a queen. A's jack of hearts is irrelevant.

Hold 'em is best played pot-limit. American casinos mostly play limit raise games, say $10 before the flop and $20 after it. This makes the game a lot less dangerous (the casinos want the players to survive, so the house can cut each pot played) but still requires very fine judgement.

British casinos (which make a session charge) always play pot-limit. If you want action, Hold 'em is where it's at.

The standard book on Hold 'em, in the sense that everyone has read it and more or less follows its recommendations and guidelines, is *Hold 'em Poker* by David Sklansky (Two Plus Two Publishing, 226 Garfield Drive, Henderson NV 89014), first published in 1977. There are a great many other books on the market but for the limit game it's probably best to continue with *Hold 'em Poker for Advanced Players* by David Sklansky and Mason Malmuth.

For no-limit, former world champion Doyle Brunson's *Super/System* (originally published as *How I Made Over $1,000,000 Playing Poker*) at $100 is a classic. It was Brunson who described no-limit Hold 'em as 'the Cadillac of poker'. But as I have mentioned in my text, you can't learn poker from books! You have to play the game and log the experience.

I should also say something about tournament poker, to elaborate my comments about it in Chapter 3. Tournaments are completely different from regular cash games. In poker tournaments, which are very popular in casino card rooms, the entry fees paid by all the players make up the total prize money, which is paid out at the end to the winners. First place usually receives 40–50%, the runner-up 25% and the other players at the *final table* smaller amounts in proportion.

The attraction of such tournaments is that for a relatively small outlay, say $25 or $50, a player can win a prize of $1,000 or often considerably more. In the World Championship, which is the biggest tournament of all, the entry costs $10,000 and first prize is a million. The next three or four players can expect pay-offs in six figures.

The style and technique of tournament play are as different from cash games as, say, one-day cricket from a regular match or speed chess from a grandmaster game. Each has its place but not every player can handle both. The best practical book on tournament play is Tom McEvoy's *Tournament Poker* (Cardsmith Publishing, 4535 West Sahara, Suite 105, Las Vegas, Nevada 89102). *Poker Tournament Strategies* by Sylvester Suzuki (Two Plus Two Publishing) offers a very technical analysis of the whole subject.

No-limit Hold 'em may well be the Cadillac of poker games but may I remind you, if you think it is easy to win a Cadillac, that it is even easier to lose one.